THE INDISPENSABLE BOOK OF
USELESS
INFORMATION

THE INDISPENSABLE BOOK OF
USELESS
INFORMATION

*Just When You Thought It Couldn't Get
Any More Useless—It Does*

DON VOORHEES

A PERIGEE BOOK

A PERIGEE BOOK
Published by the Penguin Group
Penguin Group (USA) Inc.
375 Hudson Street, New York, New York 10014, USA
Penguin Group (Canada), 90 Eglinton Avenue East, Suite 700, Toronto, Ontario M4P 2Y3, Canada
(a division of Pearson Penguin Canada Inc.)
Penguin Books Ltd., 80 Strand, London WC2R 0RL, England
Penguin Group Ireland, 25 St. Stephen's Green, Dublin 2, Ireland (a division of Penguin Books Ltd.)
Penguin Group (Australia), 250 Camberwell Road, Camberwell, Victoria 3124, Australia
(a division of Pearson Australia Group Pty. Ltd.)
Penguin Books India Pvt. Ltd., 11 Community Centre, Panchsheel Park, New Delhi—110 017, India
Penguin Group (NZ), 67 Apollo Drive, Rosedale, Auckland 0632, New Zealand
(a division of Pearson New Zealand Ltd.)
Penguin Books (South Africa) (Pty.) Ltd., 24 Sturdee Avenue, Rosebank, Johannesburg 2196, South Africa

Penguin Books Ltd., Registered Offices: 80 Strand, London WC2R 0RL, England

While the author has made every effort to provide accurate telephone numbers and Internet addresses at the time of publication, neither the publisher nor the author assumes any responsibility for errors or for changes that occur after publication. Further, the publisher does not have any control over and does not assume any responsibility for author or third-party websites or their content.

First edition: May 2011

Library of Congress Cataloging-in-Publication Data

Voorhees, Don
    The indispensable book of useless information : just when you thought it couldn't get any more useless—it does / Don Voorhees.— 1st ed.
    p.   cm.
    ISBN 978-0-399-53668-7 (trade pbk.)
    1. Curiosities and wonders. I. Title.
    AG243.V664   2011
    031.02—dc22   2011002680

PRINTED IN THE UNITED STATES OF AMERICA

10 9 8 7 6 5 4 3 2

Most Perigee books are available at special quantity discounts for bulk purchases for sales promotions, premiums, fund-raising, or educational use. Special books, or book excerpts, can also be created to fit specific needs. For details, write: Special Markets, Penguin Group (USA) Inc., 375 Hudson Street, New York, New York 10014.

Contents

MASCOT MUSINGS

The earliest squirrel species found in the fossil record dates back 40 million years.

It is believed that squirrels originated in North America.

There are ten species of squirrel in the Northern Hemisphere.

There are no squirrels in Australia.

Early spring is the hardest time of year for squirrels in temperate climates, as buried acorns and nuts have sprouted but new sources of food have not yet been produced.

Squirrels may become carnivorous when food gets scarce.

The fur of squirrels from Europe and Central Asia is used for coats, linings, and trimmings. North American squirrel skins are too sparse and coarse for such use.

Flying squirrels only come out at night. This is why they are seldom seen, even though they are widely distributed across North America.

When a squirrel flicks its tail, it is saying, "Get away!"

Squirrels can run at speeds of up to ten miles per hour.

Squirrels are frequently hit by cars because they use a strategy of darting back and forth to evade a predator. Unhappily, this often means dodging under the wheels of a vehicle.

SING A SONG

KICKSTART MY HEART

Nikki Sixx began life as Frank Carlton Ferrana Jr.

Sixx, founder and bass player for Mötley Crüe, stole his first guitar and used the money he got from selling it to buy his first bass guitar.

Sixx overdosed on heroin several times and claims he wrote the song "Kickstart My Heart" after being declared dead for two minutes and having an out-of-body experience, before EMTs revived him with a shot of adrenaline to the heart.

THE ARTIST FORMERLY KNOWN AS . . .

Prince was called Skipper as a boy.

In 1984, Prince twice had the number one movie (*Purple Rain*), the number one album (*Purple Rain*) and the number one single ("When Doves Cry" and

"Let's Go Crazy") at the same time, making him the only artist to accomplish the feat.

It was because of Prince's 1984 song "Darling Nikki" off the *Purple Rain* album that parental advisory stickers began to be placed on albums. Tipper Gore, wife of future Vice President Al Gore, heard her twelve-year-old daughter singing the song's sexually explicit lyrics and was prompted to form the Parents' Music Resource Center.

In 1994, following a dispute with Warner Bros. over the rights to his name, Prince changed it to an unpronounceable symbol which became known as Love Symbol #2.

Prince became a Jehovah's Witness in 2001 and occasionally knocks on people's doors to proselytize.

Prince was voted "World's Sexiest Vegan" by People for the Ethical Treatment of Animals in 2006.

OLD SONGS

Neil Diamond's first royalty check was for seventy-three cents, for the single "Solitary Man."

Paul Anka made $100 each time the theme song played on *The Tonight Show Starring Johnny Carson*. Anka had written the song, called "Toot Sweet," in 1959. The show ran five nights a week for thirty-two years, netting Anka $832,000 for a recycled song.

Merv Griffin's estate has earned $70 million in royalties, to date, for the *Jeopardy!* theme song, which he wrote.

OZZFEST

The first Black Sabbath album was recorded in eight hours for $1,200.

Sharon Osbourne's father, Don Arden, managed Black Sabbath. When the group dumped her husband Ozzy, Sharon took over and helped propel him to solo stardom. Her father was so resentful that the two didn't speak for twenty years.

Sharon launched the annual Ozzfest music festival in 1996, after the Lollapalooza music festival refused to allow Ozzy to perform.

In 1989, Ozzy choked Sharon until she passed out, and threatened to kill her. He was charged with making threats, but Sharon later dropped the case.

In 2007, Christina Aguilera bought the Osbournes' mansion, which was featured on their reality TV show, because she really liked the kitchen.

BEATLEMANIA

The Beatles' 1966 *Yesterday and Today* album, also known as the "Butcher Album," originally had a cover photo of the band holding bloody meat and dismembered baby dolls, to highlight the absurdity of "Beatlemania." Public reaction was so negative that the record company quickly glued new photos on the albums.

"Come Together" was written in 1969 by John Lennon for Timothy Leary's California gubernatorial bid against Ronald Reagan. Leary dropped out of the race in 1970 after he was sent to prison for possession of marijuana.

In 1973, John Lennon was sued by the publisher of Chuck Berry's song "You Can't Catch Me." "Come Together" was musically similar and shared some of the same lyrics. They settled out of court.

John Lennon wrote "Everybody's Got Something to Hide Except Me and My Monkey" about how everybody else was paranoid except him and his wife, Yoko Ono. "Monkey" was his pet name for her.

The Beatles' 1964 single "I Feel Fine" was the first rock-and-roll song to use feedback on an album. It was created when Paul McCartney held his bass up to his amp. (Earlier blues guitarists had also used the effect.)

The lyrics to "Golden Slumbers" come from a seventeenth-century lullaby poem by Thomas Dekker.

The street signs on Liverpool's Penny Lane were stolen so frequently after the Beatles wrote "Penny Lane" that the city resorted to simply painting the street name on buildings.

Sgt. Pepper's Lonely Hearts Club Band was the first album to have all the lyrics to the songs printed on the outside of the cover.

In 2000, George Harrison was stabbed by an intruder in his home and suffered a collapsed lung. His wife, Olivia, hit the guy over the head with a lamp, and his son, Dhani, held him until police arrived to arrest him.

The song title "A Hard Day's Night" came from an expression that Ringo Starr used.

Paul McCartney's 1968 song "Blackbird" was about the civil rights movement unfolding in the United States at the time.

In "Eleanor Rigby," the vicar was originally going to be called "Father McCartney," but Paul thought that would bother his dad, so he picked the name "McKenzie" out of the telephone directory.

"Hey Jude" stayed on top of the U.S. singles charts for nine weeks, the longest of any Beatles song.

George Harrison's "All Those Years Ago" was a tribute to John Lennon.

Bob Dylan first introduced the Beatles to pot in 1964.

When the Beatles played the Gator Bowl in Jacksonville, Florida, in 1964, they insisted that the audience not be segregated.

The Beatles played their last concert before a paying audience at San Francisco's Candlestick Park, in 1966.

WITH A LITTLE HELP FROM MY FRIENDS

Eric Clapton plays the guitar solo on "While My Guitar Gently Weeps."

Paul McCartney plays the kazoo on Ringo Starr's solo single "You're Sixteen."

John Lennon cowrote and did background vocals on David Bowie's number one hit "Fame."

Mick Jagger sang backup on the Beatles' "Baby You're a Rich Man."

FOUR THOUSAND HOLES

In the song "A Day in the Life," John Lennon used a story from a 1967 U.K. newspaper article about how the Blackburn Roads surveyor counted four thousand holes in the streets of Blackburn and that the amount of material required to fill them would be enough to fill Albert Hall.

The recording studio air conditioners can be heard at the very end of the forty-two-second-long last note in "A Day in the Life" as the note fades away.

John Lennon's handwritten lyrics for "A Day in the Life" sold for $1.2 million in 2010.

A guy named Mal Evans was the Beatles' road manager and was responsible for sounding the alarm clock in "A Day in the Life," banging the hammer in "Maxwell's Silver Hammer," and ringing the cow bell in "With a Little Help from My Friends." In 1976, he was killed by police responding to a domestic violence report at his home, after threatening the cops with a gun.

GET THE LED OUT

Led Zeppelin's "Stairway to Heaven" was the most requested song on FM radio stations in the United States in the 1970s, even though it was never released as a single.

In 1975, Led Zeppelin had all six of their albums on the *Billboard* Top 200.

Led Zeppelin had to cancel a 1972 show in Singapore when authorities of that nation wouldn't let them off their plane with such long hair.

Led Zeppelin was sued for plagiarizing "Whole Lotta Love," by Willie Dixon, who had written a song—"You Need Love"—with similar lyrics years earlier. They settled out of court, and future issues of the song included Dixon on songwriting credits.

ELVIS HAS LEFT THE CEMETERY

In 1976, Bruce Springsteen climbed over the wall outside of Graceland trying to meet Elvis. He was thrown out by security guards.

Also in 1976, Jerry Lee Lewis was arrested for waving a gun outside of Graceland and demanding to talk to Elvis.

In 1977, Elvis Presley's body was moved from a cemetery in Memphis, Tennessee, to Graceland after someone tried to steal it.

Though Elvis recorded the best-known version of it in 1960, "Are You Lonesome Tonight?" was first recorded in 1927 and sung by many artists before Presley, including Al Jolson.

"Heartbreak Hotel," Elvis Presley's first number one record on the pop charts, was inspired by a suicide note published in the *Miami Herald*, which read, "I walk a lonely street."

"Love Me Tender" was an adaptation of a Civil War ballad—"Aura Lee"—written in 1861.

"Can't Help Falling in Love," was based on a 1790 French ballad—"Plaisir d'Amour."

Elvis Presley's first public performance was on the back of a flatbed truck in 1954 to promote the opening of a drug store.

Elvis Presley's "Hound Dog" was the most played record on jukeboxes of all time.

Presley's daughter, Lisa Marie Presley, was married to Michael Jackson from 1994 to 1996, and to Nicolas Cage for 108 days in 2002.

THE TED COMMANDMENTS

Ted Nugent once signed a fan's arm with a Bowie knife, at the fan's request.

During the taping of the TV show *Surviving Nugent: The Ted Commandments*, Nugent accidentally cut his leg with a chain saw, requiring forty-four stitches.

WHAT A LONG STRANGE TRIP IT'S BEEN

The Grateful Dead song "Truckin'" was inspired when the band was arrested in New Orleans for possession of LSD and barbiturates.

Thirty-six people at a 1971 Grateful Dead concert were hospitalized for LSD usage.

Fifty percent of the profits from Ben & Jerry's Cherry Garcia ice cream go to the Grateful Dead's Rex Foundation.

METAL MASSACRE

Metallica's first song, "Hit the Lights," was released on a 1982 heavy metal compilation album called *Metal Massacre*.

Metallica's first solo album *Kill 'Em All* was originally going to be called *Metal Up Your Ass*, but the band's record label protested and forced the name change.

In 1986, Metallica guitarist James Hetfield broke his wrist skateboarding while on tour and had to be replaced by the band's guitar technician for the rest of the dates.

James Hetfield suffered third-degree burns when he got too close to the band's pyrotechnics at a 1992 concert.

In 1983, Metallica guitarist Dave Mustaine was fired from the band for his drug/alcohol use. He went on to form Megadeth.

Metallica was the first band to have five consecutive albums debut at number one on the *Billboard* Top 200.

BABA WHO?

The Who's "Baba O'Riley" gets its name from Meher Baba, Pete Townshend's spiritual advisor, and Terry O'Riley, an experimental musician Townshend greatly respected. The name is never mentioned in the song, and many people know it as "Teenage Wasteland." Even though it is one of the group's most popular songs, it was never released as a single.

The Who used to be known as the High Numbers.

Keith Moon died of an overdose of Hemenephirin, which he was taking to treat his alcoholism.

In 2003, Pete Townshend was cleared of possessing child pornography, but was still placed on Great Britain's sex-offender list for five years.

FOUR DEAD IN OHIO

Neil Young wrote and recorded the song "Ohio" with Crosby, Stills & Nash the day after the Kent State massacre in 1970.

Neil Young's "A Man Needs a Maid" was written about actress Carrie Snodgrass, who he had first seen in a movie and later had a child with.

At a 1999 concert at the Theater at Madison Square Garden, Neil Young was incorrectly billed as Bob Dylan.

Young wrote "Cinnamon Girl" and "Cowgirl in the Sand" in one day while sick with a fever.

Young maintains that the song "Down by the River" isn't literally about shooting his "baby," but about ruining the relationship.

CAPTAIN FANTASTIC

Songwriting partners Elton John and Bernie Taupin created nicknames for each other. Elton John is Captain Fantastic and Bernie Taupin is the Brown Dirt Cowboy. The album *Captain Fantastic and the Brown Dirt Cowboy* is a look back at their early days of writing music together.

Captain Fantastic was the first album ever to debut at number one on the U.S. pop album charts.

Elton John wrote the song "Don't Go Breaking My Heart" with Bernie Taupin under the pseudonyms Carte Blanche and Ann Orson.

Elton John left off the last verse of "Daniel," written by Bernie Taupin, about Daniel being a blind Vietnam vet who was leaving the United States for Spain, because he thought the song was too long.

The song "Someone Saved My Life Tonight" recounts Elton John's 1969 broken engagement to Linda Woodrow and the attempted suicide that followed.

Elton John's "All the Young Girls Love Alice" is about the tragic death of a sixteen-year-old lesbian who died in the streets.

Elton John was against releasing "Bennie and the Jets" as a single, thinking that it would bomb. It went to number one. Axl Rose credits the song with inspiring him to become a singer.

Elton John is the godfather of John Lennon and Yoko Ono's son Sean.

CAPTAIN JACK

The Billy Joel song "Captain Jack" is about a drug dealer in Oyster Bay, Long Island.

Billy Joel's "Allentown," which is about the city in Pennsylvania, was originally going to be called "Levittown," which is a town on Long Island.

Billy Joel played the first rock concert at Yankee Stadium in 1990.

In 1989, Billy Joel sued his manager and former brother-in-law for $90 million after discrepancies were found in an audit.

ABSOLUTELY AXL

A 1991 Guns N' Roses concert in St. Louis ended in a riot when singer Axl Rose jumped off stage to accost a fan videotaping the show.

Nirvana refused to do shows with Guns N' Roses because Kurt Cobain didn't care for Axl Rose's persona.

In 1990, Axl Rose married Erin Everly, daughter of Don Everly of the Everly Brothers. The marriage was annulled nine months later.

In 1991, a California police officer tore up a traffic ticket given to the Guns N' Roses limo driver after Axl Rose threatened to cancel that night's show in Los Angeles.

In 2006, Axl Rose was arrested in Stockholm for biting a hotel security guard on the leg.

HOT ROD

Rod Stewart used to be in a band called the Hoochie Coochie Men.

Rod Stewart was sued for kicking a soccer ball into the crowd at a 1990 concert, after a woman claimed it damaged the tendon in her middle finger, which she said made having sex with her husband difficult. She was awarded $17,000.

LIKE A BAT OUT OF HELL

The Meat Loaf song "Bat Out of Hell" is about a motorcycle crash where the rider's organs are thrown from his body—"And the last thing I see is my heart still beating/ Breaking out of my body and flying away/Like a bat out of hell."

Meat Loaf's album, *Bat Out of Hell*, still sells two hundred thousand copies a year.

SITTING ON A PARK BENCH

The homeless man in Jethro Tull's "Aqualung" has a breathing problem, which is why he was named Aqualung, after the underwater breathing apparatus.

At a 1979 concert, Jethro Tull singer Ian Anderson was injured when a fan threw a rose on stage and one of its thorns scratched his eye.

Jethro Tull keyboardist David Palmer underwent a sex-change operation in 2004.

BITTER MAN

Eddie Vedder wrote "Better Man" before he was in Pearl Jam, as a commentary on his mother marrying his step-father after his father died. He thought she settled for less of a man just to have someone to help support the family. At concerts, Vedder sometimes dedicates the song to "the bastard who married my mother."

In 2003, Pearl Jam bought 1,400 acres of jungle in Madagascar to offset the greenhouse gases that their upcoming concert tour would produce.

GO ASK ALICE

Alice Cooper was originally the name of the group, not lead singer Vincent Furnier. In 1968, Furnier adopted the name Alice Cooper.

Furnier claimed that the name came from a session on a Ouija board and that he was the reincarnation of a seventeenth-century witch by that name.

In 1977, Alice Cooper's pet boa constrictor was killed by a bite from the mouse that was supposed to be its dinner.

Cooper used to mutilate dolls on stage when he performed the song "Billion Dollar Babies."

THE BOSS

Bruce Springsteen's song "Cadillac Ranch" is about the public art display of the same name in Amarillo, Texas, where ten Cadillacs are half-buried nose first in the ground.

"Candy's Room" is about a prostitute.

Bruce Springsteen used a rhyming dictionary to write "Blinded by the Light." This was his first single, and it was a flop. Manfred Mann's Earth Band redid the song and turned it into a number one hit.

"Dancing in the Dark" is about how hard it is to write a hit song. Ironically, it became Bruce's biggest hit.

During a 1980 concert, Springsteen forgot the lyrics of "Born to Run."

MY HANDS FELT JUST LIKE TWO BALLOONS

The Pink Floyd song "Comfortably Numb" is supposedly about the time singer Roger Waters was injected with tranquilizers to ease stomach cramps, just before a 1977 concert, and was so numb that he could barely lift his arms.

In 1980, the Pink Floyd song "Another Brick in the Wall" was banned in South Africa due to rioting.

SEAL WITH A KISS

Singer Seal's birth name is Seal Henry Olusegun Olumide Adeola Samuel. Olusegun is a Yoruba name, meaning "God is victorious."

Seal's facial scars are the result of discoid lupus erythematosus, a condition where the immune cells attack the body, especially areas exposed to sunlight. Seal's scalp was also affected by this condition. He now is in remission.

Seal's 1994 song "Kiss from a Rose" originally peaked on the *Billboard* charts at number sixty. After it was used in the movie *Batman Forever*, it shot to number one.

AMERICAN IDOLS

NAME THAT CELEBRITY

Lady Gaga was born Stefani Joanne Angelina Germanotta. She created her stage name after the Queen song "Radio Ga Ga," since her vocal style is similar to that of deceased Queen singer Freddie Mercury.

Jon Stewart was born Jonathan Stuart Leibowitz.

Winona Ryder used to be Winona Laura Horowitz.

Carmen Electra dumped her old name—Tara Leigh Patrick.

Miley Cyrus was christened Destiny Hope Cyrus. Her parents expected great things from her, hence her given name. Since she smiled so much as an infant, she was given the nickname "Smiley," later shortened to "Miley."

Pat Benatar entered this world as Patricia Mae Andrzejewski.

Lil' Bow Wow began life as Shad Gregory Moss. Snoop Dogg named him "Bow Wow" after seeing him perform at age six.

Marilyn Manson is really Brian Hugh Warner.

Natalie Portman ditched her given name—Natalie Herschlag.

Michael Caine was born Maurice Micklewhite. He chose Caine for his stage name after seeing a movie marquee for *The Caine Mutiny*.

Ralph Lauren can't be blamed for dropping his given name—Ralph Reuben Lifshitz. His brother changed their last name when Ralph was sixteen.

Alan Alda was born Alphonso Joseph D'Abruzzo. He got "Alda" from combining the first two letters of his first and last names.

Chevy Chase was born Cornelius Crane Chase. His nickname, "Chevy," was given to him by his grandmother. It came from the medieval English "Ballad of Chevy Chase," which tells the story of a hunting party on a parcel of hunting land, known as a *chase*, in the Cheviot Hills, on the border of England and Scotland.

LARRY LIVE

Lawrence Harvey Zeiger is also known as Larry King.

Larry King's first celebrity interview was Bobby Darin in 1957.

PERFECT "10"

Bo Derek was born Mary Cathleen Collins.

Bo Derek began modeling at age sixteen to pay for a surfboard.

When the teen met director John Derek, thirty years her senior, he left his wife, actress Linda Evans. John Derek and Bo went off to live in Germany, where he could not be prosecuted for statutory rape.

Melanie Griffith turned down the part of Jenny in the movie *10*, which Bo Derek played. Christie Brinkley and Kim Basinger were also considered for the role.

Bo Derek's looks in the film were actually rated an eleven out of ten in the scene where the subject came up.

HELLO, DOLLY

Dolly Parton is afraid to go on the rides at her Dollywood amusement park.

Dolly's husband of forty-four years, Dean, has attended only one of her concerts.

Parton does not have children, but did raise many of her eleven siblings in their Nashville home after she married Dean.

Dolly Parton has size 40DD breasts.

In 2008, Parton had to postpone her U.S. concert tour because of back problems relating to her weighty bosom.

The first cloned animal, Dolly the sheep, was named in honor of Parton, since it was cloned from cells taken from the mammary gland of a ewe.

MESSY JESSIE

Jessica Simpson has publicly confessed to not brushing her teeth very often. She says she wipes them with her sweater.

In 2010, Simpson drank cow urine, which she promptly puked up, for an episode of VH1's reality show *The Price of Beauty*.

Even though she never smoked, Simpson likes to chew Nicorette gum.

GUESS GIRL

Anna Nicole Smith was born Vicki Lynn Hogan.

In 1985 at age seventeen, Smith married a sixteen-year-old cook from the restaurant where she was working. They had one child.

Anna Nicole Smith's odd jobs included stints at Walmart and Red Lobster, and as an exotic dancer.

In 1991, Smith answered a newspaper ad to become a *Playboy* model. She appeared on the cover of the March 1992 issue, as Vicki Smith. By 1993, she was Playmate of the Year. She weighed 155 pounds at the time, making her the heaviest Playmate of the Year ever.

Smith's weight fluctuated between 134 and 224 pounds during her life.

Smith married eighty-nine-year-old oil tycoon J. Howard Marshall in 1994 after meeting him while performing in a strip club, but never lived with him. He died thirteen months later, making her potentially very wealthy. Court cases that ensued over who should inherit Marshall's money went all the way to the U.S. Supreme Court and were ongoing in 2010.

Smith "starred" in the 1997 film *Skyscraper*, in which she plays a helicopter pilot who must rescue hostages from the top of a high-rise building.

The debut of Smith's reality show on E!, *The Anna Nicole Show*, was the highest-rated debut in that network's history.

After Smith's death in 2007, her lawyer, Howard K. Stern, claimed to be the father of her infant daughter. Later DNA testing found former boyfriend Larry Birkhead to be the dad.

YOU DON'T KNOW JACK

In addition to starring as Jack Bauer on *24*, Kiefer Sutherland has been in more than seventy movies.

Sutherland is an English-born Canadian. He was given the name Kiefer by his father, actor Donald Sutherland, as a tribute to director Warren Kiefer.

Sutherland shared a room for three years with Robert Downey Jr. when he first moved to Hollywood.

In 1990, Sutherland took a break from acting to try his hand at rodeo competition.

Sutherland was engaged to Julia Roberts in 1991. She broke it off three days before the wedding when she discovered he had been seen in the company of a stripper.

It took ten months to shoot one season of *24*.

FO' SHIZZLE

Snoop Doggy Dogg was born Cordozar Calvin Broadus. His parents nicknamed him "Snoopy" because of his looks.

Before becoming a rap star, Snoop was a Crips gang member in high school and did time for cocaine possession.

Snoop recorded songs with his cousins Nate Dogg and Lil' ½ Dead after serving his time.

Snoop Dogg is a certified football coach and served as head coach for his son's youth and high school football teams.

Snoop Dogg is banned from England and from British Airways for a 2006 incident at Heathrow Airport where his entourage was turned away from the first-class lounge (they weren't all first-class passengers) and proceeded to trash the duty-free shop and injure several police officers. He was also banned from Australia for a period of time because of his extensive criminal record.

Snoop Dogg popularized the hip-hop slang "-izzle," which had been around for many years, first being developed by black girls in Harlem to add rhyming syllables while jumping rope. Carnies have also used an "-iz" dialect for hundreds of years.

"Fo' shizzle" means "for sure" or "right on."

"Fo' shizzle, my nizzle" means "For sure, my friend."

THE LONG AND SHORT OF IT

Brooke Shields, Uma Thurman, and Jordin Sparks are all six feet tall.

Clint Eastwood, Chevy Chase, David Hasselhoff, and Conan O'Brien are all six feet, four inches tall.

Howard Stern is six foot five and Brad Garrett is six foot eight.

Mary-Kate Olsen is believed to be 4'11" (although she is officially listed as 5'1" or 5'2"). Ashley Olsen is about an inch taller than her twin sister.

Dolly Parton is five feet tall.

Hilary Duff, Nicole Richie, and Reese Witherspoon are 5'1".

Prince is 5'2".

Elton John is 5'3".

Dustin Hoffman and Fred Durst are 5'5".

GOOD *OLD* DAD

Many aging actors father children in their twilight years. Here are some celebs who might still be changing baby diapers, along with their own:

Jack Nicholson, Kevin Costner, and Mel Gibson all had babies at age fifty-four.

David Letterman had his only child at fifty-six.

Mick Jagger fathered a child at fifty-seven.

Michael Douglas had a baby with Catherine Zeta-Jones (twenty-five years his junior) at fifty-eight.

Rod Stewart did so at sixty-one and is expecting another, at the time of this writing, at age sixty-five.

Warren Beatty had one at sixty-three.

Clint Eastwood has had seven kids with five women, most recently at age sixty-five.

Good old Larry King had his last child at sixty-six.

BEFORE THEY WERE STARS

John Travolta did a TV commercial for Safeguard soap where he sang in a locker room shower with other teens.

Ben Affleck was in a Burger King ad in 1992.

Sarah Michelle Gellar also appeared in a BK ad.

Jodie Foster was in a Crest toothpaste TV ad in 1970.

Bruce Willis hawked Seagram's Golden Wine Coolers.

Brad Pitt appeared in a Pringles ad.

Keanu Reeves did a Kellogg's Corn Flakes commercial.

In 1979, Kirstie Alley won $6,000 on *Match Game*.

Vanna White was a contestant on *The Price Is Right*.

Steve Martin and Farrah Fawcett were on *The Dating Game* in 1968.

Britney Spears lost on *Star Search* in 1992.

PROJECT RUNWAY

Heidi Klum's father was a cosmetics company executive and her mother was a hairdresser. She got into modeling by winning a nationwide German modeling contest that had twenty-five thousand entrants.

> Leslie Hornby adopted the professional name Twiggy, which came from her brother Tony referring to his reed-thin sister as "Sticks."

Christie Brinkley was discovered by a photographer while at a Paris post office in 1973.

> Elle Macpherson had enrolled to study law at Sydney University in Australia before starting her modeling career in New York.

Claudia Schiffer also aspired to be a lawyer, but dropped those plans after being discovered at a disco in Düsseldorf, Germany.

> Cindy Crawford graduated high school as valedictorian and won an academic scholarship to study chemical engineering at Northwestern University, before dropping out after one semester to start modeling.

Naomi Campbell, who studied ballet, was discovered at the age of fifteen while window-shopping in London's Covent Garden.

Kate Moss was discovered at the age of fourteen while at a terminal of JFK Airport in New York.

MARRIAGE VOWS FOR $200

When Alex Trebek and his wife, Jean Currivan, exchanged wedding vows, he replied, "The answer is yes!"

LOVELY RITA

Spanish-American actress Rita Hayworth underwent electrolysis to broaden her hairline and accentuate her widow's peak, to make her appear more Northern European. She also dyed her hair red and adopted her mother's maiden name—Hayworth.

Hayworth was married and divorced five times. None of her marriages lasted more than five years.

DIVALICIOUS

Barbra Streisand is allegedly a very poor tipper. She also demands rose petals in her toilets and doesn't allow staffers to look her directly in the eyes.

Tobey Maguire is likewise said to be a notoriously bad tipper.

Jennifer Lopez once requested that a store close its doors to the public while she was shopping there. When they refused, she left a huge pile of clothes she had tried on in the dressing room and didn't buy a thing.

Will Ferrell often refuses to sign autographs.

QUEEN OF JEANS

New York socialite and designer Gloria Vanderbilt is a direct descendant of railroad and steamship magnate Cornelius Vanderbilt.

Anderson Cooper, host of CNN's *Anderson Cooper 360°*, is the son from Gloria Vanderbilt's fourth marriage, to author Wyatt Emory Cooper. Anderson Cooper appeared on *The Tonight Show* with his mother when he was just three, and began modeling for Ralph Lauren, Calvin Klein, and Macy's at ten.

In 1988, Gloria Vanderbilt's other son, Carter, jumped off the terrace of Vanderbilt's fourteenth-floor New York penthouse apartment.

Gloria Vanderbilt's tight-fitting designer jeans were the bestselling jeans of the early 1980s.

Vanderbilt is in no way associated with any products that bear her name today.

In 2009, Gloria published a novel titled *Obsession: An Erotic Tale*, which features dildos, whips, spankings, and nipple clamps.

PRYOR'S PLACE

Richard Pryor was born and raised in his grandmother's brothel, where his father pimped out his mother.

Pryor was expelled from school at age fourteen.

He served in the army from 1958 to 1960, where he spent most of his time in prison for the stabbing of a man.

Pryor briefly hosted a children's TV show in 1984 called *Pryor's Place*, which was similar to *Sesame Street*.

In 1980, he sustained burns over half of his body after freebasing cocaine and drinking 151-proof rum.

Pryor was married seven times.

REVEREND SAM

Sam Kinison was the son of two Pentecostal preachers. He followed in his parents' footsteps, becoming a preacher himself.

Kinison would do so many drugs before a show and get so worked up on stage that he kept an oxygen tank backstage to revive himself when needed.

Ironically, Kinison, who was recovering from a huge alcohol and drug problem, was killed by a seventeen-year-old drunk driver just six days after marrying his second wife.

PRINZE OF COMEDY

Freddy Prinze, comedian and father of actor Freddy Prinze Jr., was born Frederick Carl Pruetzel. He had wanted to change his last name to King, because he fancied himself the king of comedy, but Alan King already had the name, so he settled for Prinze.

DOWN AND OUT
IN BEVERLY HILLS

Kim Basinger paid $20 million to buy the town of Braselton, Georgia, and then ended up selling it for $1 million. She filed for bankruptcy in 1993, after Main Line Pictures demanded she repay $8.1 million when she backed out of starring in the movie *Boxing Helena*.

Nicolas Cage at one point owned three castles, fifteen palatial homes, two islands in the Bahamas, and a fleet of fifty sports cars. He once bought a dinosaur skull for $267,000. In 2009, he owed the IRS $6.6 million that he didn't have. Cage had earned $40 million in the previous year.

Mike Tyson made $300 million in his career, but ended up $27 million in debt. His lavish lifestyle included pet tigers. The legal fees for his divorce from Robin Givens totaled $9 million.

Michael Jackson owed $23 million on his Neverland Ranch in 2007. It cost a reported $10 million annually to operate. At the time of his death, he was reported to have about $400 million in total debt. During a few hours in the documentary *Living with Michael Jackson*, he spent $6 million on one shopping spree.

In 1990, tycoon Donald Trump was $900 million in debt.

Mark Twain went bankrupt after investing $7 million (in today's dollars) in a new typesetting machine that didn't pan out, leading to the failure of his publishing company.

Olympic figure-skating champion Dorothy Hamill filed for bankruptcy in 1996, after buying the failing Ice Capades touring company.

The comedian Sinbad owes the IRS $8.15 million. Joe Francis, the *Girls Gone Wild* guy, owes them $29.4 million, and Pamela Anderson owes $1.7 million.

Other stars who filed for bankruptcy include Burt Reynolds, Meat Loaf, Gary Coleman, Don Johnson, Mickey Rooney, and Wayne Newton.

NANNY 911

Christie Brinkley and her fourth husband, Peter Cook, split up after he was caught having an affair with the babysitter.

Sienna Miller and Jude Law broke up after he had a fling with the nanny.

Uma Thurman also got thrown over for the nanny, by Ethan Hawke, who ended up marrying her.

WITH FRIENDS LIKE THESE . . .

Denise Richards got a restraining order against ex-husband Charlie Sheen after claiming he made death threats against her.

Heather Locklear's close "friend," Richards, took up with Locklear's ex-husband Richie Sambora after they separated.

Denise Richards' father is known as Irv "Big Dicks" Richards.

EIGHTH TIME LUCKY

Liz Taylor has been married eight times to seven men. Larry King has been married eight times to seven women, but never to Liz Taylor.

THANKS FOR THE MEMORIES

Bob Hope was born in England and moved to America when he was seventeen.

One of the first vaudeville acts he performed with included the Hilton Sisters—tap dancing conjoined twins. He later did a Siamese twin dancing routine with an early partner in black face.

Hope's signature song, "Thanks for the Memories," was recorded for the 1938 film *The Big Broadcast of 1938*, in which he plays a divorced man reminiscing about the good times of his failed marriage.

Bob Hope logged 8 million air miles flying overseas with USO tours to entertain American troops.

He was honored by the U.S. Congress in 1996, when they declared him "the first and only honorary veteran of the U.S. Armed Forces."

FEAR FACTOR

Tyra Banks is terrified of dolphins.

Orlando Bloom is afraid of pigs.

Bobby Brown can't stand dogs or heights.

Sean "Diddy" Combs suffers from coulrophobia—the fear of clowns.

Carmen Electra, the *Baywatch* babe, is afraid of water, as are Michelle Pfeiffer and Winona Ryder.

Megan Fox can't bear to touch paper, use silverware in a restaurant, or sit on a public toilet.

Nicole Kidman gets nervous around butterflies.

Madonna hates thunder.

Matthew McConaughey avoids revolving doors.

Oprah can't stand chewed gum.

Christina Ricci is grossed out by houseplants.

Billy Bob Thornton gets queasy around antiques.

INSIDE HOLLYWOOD

I'LL BE THERE FOR YOU

Téa Leoni was the *Friends* producers' first choice for Rachel.

Leah Remini auditioned for the part of Monica. Janeane Garofalo was offered the part, but turned it down.

Jennifer Aniston's father, John Aniston, plays Victor Kiriakis on *Days of Our Lives*.

Each "friend" started the show making $22,500 per episode and ended up earning $1 million per episode.

Courteney Cox was the only regular cast member never to get an Emmy nomination.

MOVIN' ON UP

The Jeffersons was a spin-off of *All in the Family*.

The building shown at the beginning of the show is located at 185 East 85th Street in Manhattan.

123 SESAME STREET

Sesame Street was originally going to be called *123 Avenue B.*

Cookie Monster once revealed that, before having his first cookie, his name was Sid.

Originally, the Carpenters tune "Sing a Song" was going to be the show's theme song.

In very early episodes, Barkley was called Woof Woof.

I'LL BE BACK

Before casting Arnold Schwarzenegger to play the lead in *The Terminator*, the producers had wanted O.J. Simpson. Director James Cameron said no way—he seemed too nice!

Arnold's trademark line in the movie, "I'll be back," was originally written in the script as "I'll come back."

Cameron later married actress Linda Hamilton, who played Sarah Connor.

Cameron has been married five times, including to one of his producers and two of his actresses.

Cameron did the charcoal sketching of Kate Winslet in the famous *Titanic* nude scene.

BLUE PEOPLE

"Avatar" is Sanskrit for "incarnation." Hindu scriptures use the word to describe human incarnations of God.

Director James Cameron hired linguist Paul R. Frommer to create a new language of about one thousand words—called Na'vi—for the movie *Avatar*.

Sigourney Weaver wore a Stanford tank top in much of the film as a nod to her having attended that school.

James Cameron did not invent the word "unobtainium." The term has been used in engineering circles since the late 1950s to refer to any ideal material with special properties that either does not exist, or is extremely difficult to acquire.

YOU'LL SHOOT YOUR EYE OUT, KID

The holiday classic, *A Christmas Story*, was based in part on a series of stories by Jean Sheppard that ran in *Playboy* magazine between 1964 and 1966.

The movie inspired the television series *The Wonder Years*.

Jack Nicholson was considered for the role of "The Old Man"—Ralphie's father.

Peter Billingsley, who played Ralphie, was a co-host of the TV show *Real People*.

In the scene where Flick's tongue is frozen to the flag-pole, a hidden suction tube was used to hold the tongue in place.

One can buy a full-size replica of the film's iconic leg lamp at the Christmas Story House gift shop in Cleveland.

MAD AS A HATTER

Charles Lutwidge Dodgson was the given name of Lewis Carroll, author of *Alice's Adventures in Wonderland* and *Through the Looking-Glass*.

In *Alice's Adventures in Wonderland*, the Mad Hatter asks Alice, "Why is a raven like a writing desk?" Lewis Carroll admitted he never came up with a good answer to this riddle. (Some wits now suggest the answer is Edgar Allan Poe, who worked on both.)

Lindsay Lohan campaigned unsuccessfully for the role of Alice in Tim Burton's film adaptation.

OOMPA-LOOMPAS

The 1971 movie *Willy Wonka and the Chocolate Factory*, starring Gene Wilder, was based on the 1964 Roald Dahl novel, *Charlie and the Chocolate Factory*. The Quaker Oats Company, who financed the film, had the title changed to help promote the new Willy Wonka candy they were introducing. Also, at the time, the word "Charlie" was used as a derogatory term for the Vietcong.

> Dahl was so disappointed with the film that he prohibited any future versions of *Charlie and the Chocolate Factory* to be produced while he was still alive.

The chocolate river in the Chocolate Room was made by adding chocolate ice cream mix to 150,000 gallons of water.

> Julie Dawn Cole, who played Veruca Salt, hated chocolate.

Many of the chocolate bars used in the movie were made of wood.

> The producers had to go outside of Germany, the country the film was shot in, to find little people to play the Oompa-Loompas, since so many of them had been exterminated by the Nazis.

I'LL HAVE WHAT SHE'S HAVING

Katz's Deli on East Houston Street in New York City is where Meg Ryan memorably faked an orgasm for Billy Crystal while sitting at the table in *When Harry Met Sally*.

The table where the scene was shot now has a plaque that reads, "Congratulations! You are sitting where Sally met Harry."

Director Rob Reiner's mother is the lady who quips, "I'll have what she's having," after Ryan's fake orgasm.

MRS. ROBINSON, YOU'RE TRYING TO SEDUCE ME

In *The Graduate*, Dustin Hoffman, who played Benjamin, was only six years younger than Anne Bancroft, who played the seductive Mrs. Robinson.

La Verne United Methodist Church is the setting where Dustin Hoffman's character pounds on the glass at the rear of the church to try and stop Katherine Ross (Elaine) from getting married.

The hit Simon & Garfunkel song "Mrs. Robinson," was originally going to be called "Mrs. Roosevelt." Paul Simon had not written it for the movie soundtrack, but director Mike Nichols liked it so much that he had Simon change the title.

I'M AN EXCELLENT DRIVER!

In the movie *Rain Man*, Dustin Hoffman, who played Raymond, was originally supposed to play the part of Charlie Babbitt. Hoffman had wanted Bill Murray to play the part of Charlie.

Robert De Niro and Jack Nicholson turned down the role of Raymond Babbitt.

Many airlines deleted the scene from their in-flight movies where Raymond recites the statistics of air travel disasters. Qantas, however, did not. (They were mentioned in the film as being the only airline never to have had a fatal crash.)

In the film, Raymond memorized a phone book up to Marsha and William Gottsegen, the names of Hoffman's real life in-laws.

The sales of the style of Ray-Ban sunglasses worn by Tom Cruise in the film shot up 15 percent after its release.

LIFE IS LIKE A BOX OF CHOCOLATES

John Travolta, Bill Murray, and Chevy Chase all were considered for the role of Forrest in *Forrest Gump*.

The Vietnam scenes were shot in South Carolina.

Jim Hanks, Tom Hanks' younger brother, was his body double in many of the running scenes.

Tom Hanks' real-life daughter, Elizabeth, is the red-haired girl on the school bus.

Dave Chappelle and Ice Cube both turned down the part of Bubba.

Gary Sinise, who played Lieutenant Dan, had his legs covered with a special blue fabric in the wheelchair scenes so they could be optically removed later.

NAPALM IN THE MORNING

George Lucas was originally supposed to direct *Apocalypse Now*.

Harvey Keitel had the role of Captain Willard for the first two weeks of the movie's filming, and then was replaced by Martin Sheen, after artistic differences with director Francis Ford Coppola.

Martin Sheen really *was* drunk in the hotel room scene when he punches the mirror. He was so drunk, he even went after Coppola.

Martin Sheen had a heart attack while filming in the Philippines, and his brother, Joe Estevez, was flown in to act as a double while he was in the hospital. Coppola hid the heart attack from the studio for fear that they would pull the plug on the project. Estevez was also brought in during postproduction to do voiceovers of Sheen, because Sheen was too busy to do them.

Marlon Brando showed up for filming intoxicated, terribly overweight, and with no knowledge of his lines. Coppola had to change the script to make Brando's Kurtz character massive, as opposed to skinny. He was shot in shadow to obscure the deplorable shape he was in.

Much of the movie's dialogue was overdubbed in postproduction because background noises made it unintelligible.

A real water buffalo was actually slaughtered in one scene.

The movie was supposed to be shot in a month and a half, but after a typhoon destroyed the sets and other delays, it took sixteen months to complete.

The movie has no opening credits. The title is seen as scrawled graffiti later in the film.

TOO BLOODY REAL

The battle scenes in *Saving Private Ryan* were so realistic that the Department of Veterans Affairs set up a special 800 phone number to help former soldiers who were disturbed by the movie.

Real amputees were used in the scenes where soldiers' limbs are blown off. They had prosthetic limbs fitted that were removed to create the illusion.

The opening battle scene required forty barrels of fake blood.

Director Steven Spielberg used 2,500 members of the Irish armed forces as extras.

Saving Private Ryan is said to be George W. Bush's favorite movie.

HOUSTON, WE HAVE A PROBLEM

Brad Pitt and John Travolta turned down starring roles in *Apollo 13*.

The cast and crew made more than five hundred parabolic-arc flights on NASA's KC-135 airplane, which creates zero gravity conditions for a period of twenty-three seconds, while filming the weightless space scenes.

In real life, Tom Hanks—at six feet, one inch—would be too tall by an inch to be an astronaut.

Director Ron Howard's mother made a cameo as Blanche Lovell, and his father played a priest.

INDIANA SMITH?

Indiana Jones was called Indiana Smith right up until the first day of filming of *Raiders of the Lost Ark*.

Steve Martin, Chevy Chase, and Bill Murray were all considered to play the role of Indiana Jones.

The scene where Indy shoots the sword-wielding Arab was changed on the set. Harrison Ford and the crew had food poisoning. Ford needed to get to a bathroom urgently and decided to just shoot him and get it over with.

Director Steven Spielberg ate mostly cans of SpaghettiOs while filming in Tunisia. This may account for the fact that he was the only member of the cast or crew not to get sick on location.

The sound of thousands of slithering snakes was created by the sound designer sticking his fingers into a cheese casserole.

The sound of the heavy lid on the ark being slid back was created by sliding the porcelain lid off a toilet tank.

Indy's whip is ten feet long.

DÉJÀ VU, ALL OVER AGAIN

In *Groundhog Day*, Bill Murray is supposed to have relived the same day for ten years, according to director Harold Ramis. Parts of thirty-eight different days are depicted.

Bill Murray was bitten twice by the groundhog during the filming of the movie.

BUILD IT AND THEY WILL COME

The actual ball field built on a corn farm used to film *Field of Dreams* is now a tourist attraction in Dyersville, Iowa. It draws sixty-five thousand visitors a year.

There was a drought during the shooting of the movie, and the grass had to be painted green, since it had turned so brown.

The owners of the farm were paid $50,000 by Universal Studios for location shooting.

In 2010, the 163-acre property was put up for sale with an asking price of $5.4 million.

SORE WINNER

George C. Scott refused his 1970 Best Actor Academy Award for the movie *Patton*, saying the Oscars were a "two-hour meat parade," and quipping that if Marlon Brando did not win for *Streetcar Named Desire*, he shouldn't for *Patton*.

THAT'S ALL, FOLKS

Mel Blanc did the voices for Bugs Bunny, Daffy Duck, Foghorn Leghorn, Sylvester the Cat, Tweety Bird, Woody Woodpecker, Porky Pig, Yosemite Sam, Pepe LePew, Speedy Gonzales, the Tasmanian Devil, Marvin the Martian, Wile E. Coyote, Mr. Spacely, Frito Bandito, Barney Rubble, and Dino the Dinosaur. He also did vocal effects for Tom Cat and Jerry Mouse.

Blanc would actually chomp on carrots while doing his Bugs Bunny voicing.

Mel Blanc's epitaph reads, "That's all, folks!"

EGGHEAD TV

C-SPAN is short for Cable-Satellite Public Affairs Network.

> C-SPAN is owned by the cable television industry and accepts no advertising. It is in no way connected to the government.

C-SPAN does not receive Nielsen ratings.

BUSINESS REPORT

LOST IN TRANSLATION

Some products sold in other countries have names that are quite humorous in English. A few examples follow:

Entenmann's baked goods and Thomas' English Muffins are owned by Bimbo Bakeries USA, the largest bakery company in the United States. It is in turn owned by Mexican company, Grupo Bimbo. The word "Bimbo" was made up. It means nothing in Spanish.

Fart Juice is sold in Poland. The word *fart* means "luck" in Polish.

JussiPussi rolls are marketed in Finland. "Jussi" is the name of the man who started the company and *pussi* means "bag" in Finnish.

Pee Cola can be found in Ghana.

Plopp chocolate candy bars are available in the Czech Republic.

Big Nuts chocolate bars are enjoyed in Belgium.

Cock Soup is slurped in Jamaica.

Dickmilch is a German sour milk drink. *Dick* means "thick" in German.

Erektus energy drink is from Slovakia.

Vergina Beer is quaffed in Greece.

Shito Mix is an African seasoning.

Prick potato chips are made in Brazil.

Coming Lemon is a Japanese candy.

Creamy Balls is another Japanese candy.

Fingering Marie is a Swedish cookie.

Crap's chocolate is a hit in France.

Spotted Dick is an English sponge cake made by Heinz.

Pimp Juice is an American product marketed as "Hip-Hop's #1 Energy Drink."

Ass Glue is a Chinese product.

Sticky Ass Glue is made in the good ol' USA.

DRIVEN TO SUCCEED

During the height of their production in the 1920s, there was a new Ford Model-T coming off the production line every twenty-four seconds.

When the Model-T first came out in 1908, so few people knew how to drive that the cars came with instructions.

KING OF CARS

Hyundai is the world's leading automaker by profit, and is also the world's fastest-growing car company.

Hyundai means "modernity" in Korean.

The company logo—a stylized "H"—is said to represent the customer and the company shaking hands.

Hyundais were first sold in the United States in 1986.

In 2006, the head of the company was arrested for embezzling $106 million.

Kia was acquired by Hyundai in 1998. The word "Kia" means "rising out of Asia," according to the company.

TOYODA

Toyota was founded by the Toyoda family in 1937. The company name is spelled differently because the word "Toyota" is thought to have a luckier number of brush strokes when written in Japanese.

Toyoda literally means "fertile rice paddies" in Japanese, and a more modern name was desired that wouldn't evoke the image of old-fashioned farming.

Toyota is the largest automaker in the world and the top-selling brand in the United States.

BEST BUYS

According to the 2010 J.D. Power and Associates Initial Quality Study, the automaker with the fewest new car problems was Porsche, followed by Acura, Mercedes-Benz, Lexus, and Ford.

BAD INVESTMENT

In two years, a Rolls-Royce loses 50 percent of its value.

IN THE MOOD

The mood ring, which was said to tell the emotions of the wearer by changing color, was invented by jeweler Marvin Wernick, in 1975. It was popularized by Joshua Reynolds, heir to the R.J. Reynolds tobacco fortune, who also invented the ThighMaster.

The rings were filled with a thermochromic liquid crystal that would vary in color according to temperature. The ring's crystals were calibrated to have a green or blue color at 82°F, the average person's normal resting peripheral temperature. Feeling happy or romantic causes skin temperatures to rise, which gave the ring a violet color. When one becomes excited or stressed, skin temperatures drop, which resulted in the crystal color changing to yellow. Anxiety or fear produced a brown or black color.

In 2010, a "mood lipstick" hit the market. Mood Swing Emotionally Activated Lip Gloss goes on clear but changes to crimson red when the wearer is feeling frisky. Changes in body chemistry cause the color to deepen. A color chart comes with each tube to determine the degree of excitement.

SNAP, CRACKLE, POP

Bubble Wrap debuted in 1960 and was originally envisioned as a new type of textured wallpaper.

It is created by trapping air between sheets of plastic after they pass over rollers, which make the indentations.

The last Monday in January is Bubble Wrap Appreciation Day.

BEFORE ITS TIME

Luther Simjian invented the first ATM in 1939. It was tested in New York City by the City Bank of New York (now Citicorp), but it died a quiet death due to lack of interest by customers. The only people who used the cash machine were prostitutes and gamblers who didn't want to deal with bank tellers.

PHONY FACTS

The true inventor of the telephone was a Staten Island resident, Italian Antonio Meucci, in 1856, twenty years before Alexander Graham Bell got his patent. Meucci never filed a patent for his invention, but Bell did so in 1876.

Bell's company—AT&T—would employ one million people by 1974.

CAN YOU HEAR ME NOW?

The first mobile phone was installed by Lars Mangus Ericsson, who founded the Ericsson phone company, when he put a phone in his car. Ericsson had long wires attached to the phone and could run them out to any nearby telephone wires.

The first cell phone call was made by Dr. Martin Cooper, of Motorola, in 1973 on the streets of New York City.

The cell phone business receives the most consumer complaints, followed by the cable/satellite TV business and banks.

SLICK PRODUCT

WD-40 stands for "water displacement—40th attempt." Inventor Norm Larsen came up with the concoction that displaces standing water to prevent corrosion in 1953 on his fortieth try.

WD-40 was originally used to coat the outer skin of Atlas missiles to prevent rust and corrosion.

Only four people know the secret formula to WD-40.

SOME ASSEMBLY REQUIRED

IKEA, the world's largest furniture retailer, was founded by seventeen-year-old Swede Ingvar Kamprad in 1943.

> IKEA is an acronym of the founder's name (Ingvar Kamprad), the farm he grew up on (Elmtaryd), and his home parish in Sweden (Agunnaryd).

BROADCAST YOURSELF

YouTube was created by three guys working at PayPal—Steve Chen, Chad Hurley, and Jawed Karim—in 2005, after Karim became frustrated about not being able to easily find a video clip of Janet Jackson's Super Bowl halftime wardrobe malfunction.

COME FLY WITH ME

Continental Airlines began as Varney Speed Lines, an airmail and passenger carrier in the Southwest in 1934.

> The airline's founder, Walter T. Varney, also founded United Airlines. United began as Varney Airlines in 1925, providing airmail service in the Pacific Northwest.

Delta Air Lines was the world's biggest carrier before the merger of United Airlines and Continental Airlines in 2010.

Delta began in 1924 as Huff Daland Dusters, a crop-dusting business in Macon, Georgia.

American Airlines was formed by an amalgamation of several smaller airlines in 1930.

In 2009, airlines based in the United States made an additional $7.8 billion by charging for extra baggage, as well as fees for changing reservations and for pets and children traveling alone.

🌰 FINDERS KEEPERS

Much of the baggage lost on American airlines ends up in the Unclaimed Baggage Center in Scottsboro, Alabama, where it is sold in a retail store and through eBay. Over one million items pass through the center in a year. Some of the more unusual unclaimed items included a 40-carat emerald, a full suit of armor, and Egyptian artifacts from 1500 BC.

24/7

The Japanese-owned 7-Eleven store chain is the largest in the world. With almost thirty-seven thousand stores, it passed McDonald's in 2007.

7-Eleven began as Tote'm Stores in Dallas in 1927.

In 1946, Tote'm adopted new extended hours—7 a.m. to 11 p.m.—hence the name change.

There are more than fifteen hundred 7-Elevens in Tokyo.

SMOKING LETTUCE

In the late 1980s, R.J. Reynolds spent $1 billion developing a smokeless cigarette marketed as the Premier. Unfortunately it tasted like burnt lettuce and was pulled from shelves in less than a year.

FIVE-FINGER DISCOUNT

The most commonly shoplifted items at the local supermarket are health and beauty supplies, followed closely by meat. Liquor, razor blades, and baby formula round out the top five.

FRUGAL TIMES

In 2009, 55 percent of American consumers said that they were buying more items on sale, up from 48 percent in 2006.

MOVE OVER, WARREN

In 2010, Mexican telecommunications (cell phone companies) magnate, Carlos Slim, became the richest person in the world, besting Warren Buffett and Bill Gates, who both gave away billions to charity. According to *Forbes*, Slim was worth $53.5 billion in early 2010.

In 2006, Warren Buffett pledged to give away 10 million shares of Berkshire Hathaway stock to the Bill & Melinda Gates Foundation, estimated to be worth about $30 billion at the time.

In 2006, Buffett paid 19 percent of his income in federal taxes, while his employees paid 33 percent of theirs.

APRIL FOOL

Steve Jobs and Steve Wozniak created the video game *Breakout*, before leaving Atari to start Apple, on April 1, 1976.

Apple had three founders—Jobs, Wozniak, and a guy named Ron Wayne. Wayne drew up the company's charter, designed the original logo, and wrote the manual for the Apple I computer. Wayne, who was forty-two at the time, twice the age of the other two, also had a 10 percent stake in the company. He sold out his share for just eight hundred dollars twelve days later, afraid the venture would flop and creditors would seize his assets. Had he held on to his share of the company, it would have been worth $22 billion in 2010.

Today, Wayne lives off his Social Security checks and what he makes selling coins and stamps from his home.

In 2010, Wayne, who has never owned an Apple product, bought his first computer—a Dell.

PIZZA AND PONG

Atari founder Nolan Bushnell also founded Chuck E. Cheese as a place kids could go to eat pizza and play video games.

RUNAWAY SUCCESS

The owner of Segway Inc.—James Heselden—died in 2010 when he rode his Segway off a cliff at his English estate.

VIRGINS

Richard Branson founded Virgin Records as a small mail order business in London in 1970. He originally would buy unsold records returned to the distributor, and sell them out of the trunk of his car, before later selling them through mail order.

In 1971, Branson opened a record store known as Virgin Records. The name was taken from the fact that he was a "virgin," at the time, when it came to business.

He used the profits from the store, in 1972, to buy a recording studio, and his record company was born after signing acts such as the Sex Pistols and Culture Club.

Branson sold Virgin Records in 1992 for $1 billion to help keep his fledgling Virgin Airlines afloat.

Branson's "Virgin" branding went on to include TV stations, cars, cosmetics, "green" fuels, hotels, books, trains, vodka, a rugby team, mobile communications, health clubs, a Formula 1 racing team, and umbilical cord stem cell banks.

FABULOUS FLOPS

The development costs (in today's dollars) for some of the business world's biggest flops:

Ford's Edsel—$2.2 billion

Apple's Newton (an early PDA platform)—$1.5 billion

Sony's Betamax—$400 million

McDonald's Arch Deluxe—$350 million

Coca-Cola's New Coke—$200 million

RISKY BUSINESS

Lloyd's of London is not an insurance company, but a society of underwriters who come together to pool and spread out risk.

Lloyd's began in 1688 at Edward Lloyd's coffee-house in London, where merchants and ship owners would gather to discuss insurance deals among themselves.

Between 1688 and 1807, much of the insurance arranged through Lloyd's was for slave-trading ships.

Lloyd's will underwrite many unusual policies that other insurers won't touch, including kidnap-and-ransom insurance, Brooke Shields's legs, Keith Richards's fingers, America Ferrera's smile, and Jimmy Durante's nose.

A LITTLE SHORT

Andrew Carnegie was just five feet, three inches tall.

PRICE DOES NOT INCLUDE . . .

Those commercial disclaimer voice guys talk so fast because, not only are they speaking quickly, but the gaps between words and syllables are digitally removed.

HARD AT WORK?

The average American worker looks at two thousand web pages a month while on the job, wasting about two hours a day.

Employees in the private sector take 7.4 sick days a year, compared to government workers, who take 10.2 sick days.

The average American lunch break is thirty-five minutes.

The typical unemployed person in the United States spends eighteen whole minutes a day looking for work.

Twelve thousand sheets of paper are used each year for every worker in the United States.

An Australian study recently found that blond women earn 7 percent more than non-blondes and are more likely to marry rich men. It didn't explain why.

ENERGIZED

In the two years after Thomas Edison developed his lightbulb, his company built five thousand electric power stations.

MADOFF WITH THE MONEY

Bernie Madoff, perpetrator of the biggest Ponzi scheme in history, got started in investing as a penny stock trader, using $5,000 he had saved from jobs as a lifeguard and installing sprinklers.

Madoff served on the boards of several charitable foundations that trusted him with their endowments. Many of these nonprofit organizations went belly up after his investment scandal was revealed.

He was a very generous philanthropist, giving away millions of dollars (of other people's money) to charity.

Madoff donated close to $200,000 to Democratic candidates and roughly $30,000 to Republicans. New York Senator Chuck Schumer returned $30,000 to the bankruptcy trustee overseeing the case.

Madoff's fifty-five foot yacht was named *Bull*.

Madoff had four homes that were each worth more than $30 million.

The Palm Beach Country Club, where he trolled for victims, charged a $300,000 initiation fee.

One of those duped by Madoff was Stephen Greenspan, author of the book *Annals of Gullibility*. He lost $400,000.

Madoff is now serving a 150-year sentence at a federal correctional facility in North Carolina, where he will be eligible for parole in 2139.

The amount of investor funds found to be missing was $21 billion, about half of which is still unaccounted for.

As the World Turns

NAUGHTY NAMES

Great Britain has some of the more interesting place-names in the English-speaking world:

Cockhaven is a region in Devon, England.

Titup Hall Drive is in Oxfordshire. (*Titup* means "prancing horse.")

Tom Tits Lane, in Somerton, is named for a type of bird.

Hardon Road is found in Wolverhampton.

Lord Hereford's Knob is located in Wales.

Shitterton is a hamlet in Dorset.

Twatt is a place-name in the Orkneys and in Shetland, England. (*Twatt* means "small parcel of land" in Old Norse.)

Not to be outdone, the town of Fucking, Austria, is named after sixth-century nobleman Lord Fucko.

ONE WORLD

Franklin Delano Roosevelt first coined the term "United Nations," when referring to the Allies in World War II. He put together the Atlantic Charter, in 1942, a body devoted to pressing on with the war.

The United Nations (U.N.) officially formed in 1945 and first convened in London.

Today's U.N. headquarters was built in 1949 with a $65 million interest-free loan from the United States. France, the Netherlands, and the United Kingdom all were against locating the U.N. in America.

The U.N. specifies British usage and Oxford Dictionary spelling for English.

The Hague, in the Netherlands, is the seat of the United Nations' judicial branch.

The United States contributes 22 percent of the U.N. budget.

In 2010, Libya, whose record on human rights Amnesty International describes as "dire," was elected to the United Nations Human Rights Council.

SPLITTER UPPERS

A thriving business in Japan is the *wakaresaseya*, which means "splitter upper." These professionals are hired by parents to seduce away unsuitable lovers of a son or daughter. They also are hired by wives to seduce away mistresses from their husbands, or to get spouses to cheat and use this as evidence against them in divorce proceedings.

Professionals in this business claim that men are the easier target and that almost any man can be seduced by an attractive female *wakaresaseya*.

NORSE POWER

Between 1825 and 1925, one-third of Norway's population moved to the United States.

Norway gets 99 percent of its energy from hydropower.

By law in Norway, 40 percent of a corporation's board of directors must be women.

PYRAMID POWER

The Great Pyramid of Giza is made of an estimated 2.3 million blocks of massive stone.

Built circa 2560 BC, the pyramid remained the tallest manmade structure (about 480 feet) for over 3,800 years.

PAPAL POWER

The Pope is Europe's last absolute monarch.

The Vatican became an independent nation in 1929.

The ATMs in Vatican City are in Latin.

There are thirty miles of bookshelves in the Vatican's Secret Archives.

MOVIE MADMAN

Kim Jong-il, the leader of North Korea, is afraid of flying and travels by armored train.

Kim is a big movie fan, with a collection of twenty thousand films. His favorites reportedly are *Godzilla*, *Rambo*, *Friday the 13th*, and James Bond movies. He also appears to adore Elizabeth Taylor.

In 1978, Kim had South Korean movie actress Choi Eun-hee kidnapped in Hong Kong. When her husband, critically acclaimed movie director Shin Sang-ok, went to Hong Kong to investigate, he too was kidnapped. Kim used the pair to build a North Korean movie industry. Shin directed several movies while in North Korea, with Kim acting as executive producer, one very similar to *Godzilla*. Shin and Choi escaped in 1986.

MONEY MATTERS

The currency of Sweden is the *krona*. The currency of Denmark and Norway is the *krone*. The currency of Iceland is the *króna*.

The largest banknote ever printed was the Philippine one-hundred-thousand-peso note. It was the size of a sheet of legal paper and was offered to collectors only.

GDP is short for "gross domestic product." It is the value of everything produced in a country during a specific time. GNP (gross national product) is the value of everything produced by a country during a specific period of time, plus earnings from abroad.

In 2010, a wealthy, Ferrari-driving Swiss man received a $290,000 speeding ticket. Many European countries adjust traffic fines to the income of the scofflaw.

FROM HERE TO TIMBUKTU

Monrovia, Liberia, is the only non-American capital city named after an American president—James Monroe, who had freed slaves sent there.

The land at the southernmost tip of England is called Land's End. (The clothing company is Lands' End.)

Timbuktu is a town in Mali, a country in West Africa.

The former Saigon is now known as Ho Chi Minh City.

From 1841 to 1848, the Yucatán Peninsula in Mexico was a sovereign nation called the Republic of Yucatán.

UNCLE SANTA

Santa Claus is known as "Grandfather Frost" in Russia. They call him "Father Christmas" in England, "Pere Noel" in France, and "Santa no ojsan" (Uncle Santa) in Japan.

Traditional Ukrainians put a spiderweb on their Christmas tree for good luck.

CAN YOU SPELL THAT?

Llanfairpwllgwyngyllgogerychwyrndrobwll-llantysiliogogogoch is a village in Wales that has the longest place-name in Europe. The name is Welsh for "St. Mary's Church in a hollow of white hazel near the swirling whirlpool of the church of St. Tysilio with a red cave." The name was conceived as a publicity stunt in the 1860s to attract tourism.

HIGHWAY FROM HELL

The most dangerous road in the world in 2004 was the highway from downtown Baghdad to the airport. An armored-taxi ride at the time cost $5,000.

One half of the traffic accidents in the developed world involve pedestrians.

Traffic accidents are the most common cause of non-natural death for Americans in foreign countries.

A WALL TO KEEP PEOPLE OUT

The Great Wall of China is *not* visible from space with the naked eye.

Rather than being one continuous wall, the Great Wall is a series of several walls that were built over a period of two thousand years.

The wall that exists today was built by the Ming dynasty. Most earlier walls have fallen into disrepair or have totally eroded away.

The slaves who died building the wall are rumored to have been buried within.

A WALL TO KEEP PEOPLE IN

The Berlin Wall, which encircled West Berlin, was erected without warning in a single night in 1961.

Between 1961 and its fall in 1989, about five thousand people tried to scale the wall. An estimated two hundred were gunned down.

The last person to die trying to escape from East Germany was Winfried Freudenberg in 1989, when the homemade balloon he used crashed in West Berlin.

The last person to be shot while trying to scale the Wall was Chris Gueffroy, in 1989. The guards who killed him were given an award and a cash bonus.

TILTED TOWER

The Leaning Tower of Pisa was built as a church bell tower. It was constructed in three phases, the lower portion being completed in 1173. The lower section began to lean to the southwest almost as soon as it was completed, due to an unstable substrate and poor foundation design. The second phase of the construction began in 1272. Because of the leaning base, the middle section was built with one side taller than the other to compensate, giving the tower a curved appearance.

The bell tower at the top was not finished until 1372.

There are seven bells in the tower, one for each note of the musical scale.

Between 1990 and 2001, remedial action was taken to halt the progression of its tilt and straighten it back to a tilt of 3.99 degrees, up from a tilt of 5.5 degrees. Engineers were careful not to straighten the tower back to perpendicular, since tourists want to see a *leaning* tower.

There are also several other towers in Pisa that are leaning.

A DEVIL OF A PLACE

The notorious French penal colony—Devil's Island—was created by Emperor Napoleon III in 1852 and remained open until 1952. The facility was actually a number of prisons located on three islands and the mainland of French Guiana.

Most of the eighty thousand inmates sent to the colony were never seen again. Those who completed their sentences were required to live in Guiana for periods of time equal to their original sentences.

The most famous inmate associated with Devil's Island—Henri Charrière—wrote the bestselling novel *Papillon*. Most of the adventures in the book were taken from other prisoner's stories or were simply made up. Charrière never actually did time on Devil's Island, but escaped from a prison on the mainland.

BURN, BABY, BURN

Underground coal fires in China burn 109 million tons of coal a year, releasing as much carbon dioxide into the atmosphere as all the cars and light trucks in the United States.

Burning Mountain in Australia has a coal fire beneath it that has been burning for an estimated six thousand years.

Canada uses more barrels of petroleum a year per capita than does the United States.

RUN IT UP THE FLAGPOLE

The modern Canadian flag—red and white with the maple leaf—was adopted in 1965. Previous flags featured Britain's Union Jack.

Nepal's double-triangle-shaped flag is the only national flag that is not quadrilateral.

The large star on the Chinese flag represents the Communist Party and the four smaller stars represent the four social classes— the working class, the peasantry, the urban petty bourgeoisie, and the national bourgeoisie.

Flags are flown at half-mast (or half-staff) to symbolize something above the flag, generally regarded as the "invisible flag of death."

SWORN VIRGINS

In rural Albania and Bosnia, some women in families with no male heirs become "sworn virgins." They must become celibate and live their lives dressing and acting like men. This is traditionally the only way a woman can inherit property, a business, or a family name.

ARE YOU DEAD YET?

In parts of Indonesia, families keep the corpse of a dead relative in an open casket in their homes until they are able to afford a proper burial. In some cases, this may take months or years, and the family acts as if the corpse is still alive, even bringing it three meals a day.

THAT'S A MOUTHFUL

Queen Elizabeth II's formal title is Elizabeth the Second, by the Grace of God, of the United Kingdom of Great Britain and Northern Ireland and Her Other Realms and Territories, Queen Head of the Commonwealth, Defender of the Faith. (That's a little long to put on her letterhead, though.)

NOBEL STUDENTS

Sixty-three Nobel laureates went to the University of Cambridge.

Forty-nine percent of college students at the University of Cambridge admit to cheating.

IRAN AWAY

Women in Iran need their husbands' consent to get a passport.

A wife cannot leave the house without her husband's permission.

Women caught out in public without a hijab (head covering) are subject to seventy-four lashes.

In Iran, it is illegal for women to have a tan. This is because the powers that be believe it distracts young men and causes earthquakes.

Article 209 of Iran's constitution says that a woman is only equal to half a man. If a man kills a woman, her family must pay the killer's family money to compensate them for *their* loss, if he is to be dismembered or executed. Also, in court proceedings, a man's testimony is equal to that of two women.

Female health care is totally segregated from male health care in Iran, and only female doctors can treat female patients. Unfortunately there is a serious shortage of women doctors.

In 2010, the United Nations (in its infinite wisdom) elected Iran to be a member of the Commission on the Status of Women—a body that is charged with helping to protect the rights of women.

In 1988, Ayatollah Khomeini issued a fatwa to kill Salman Rushdie, the author of the novel *The Satanic Verses* and the publishers of the book. While Rushdie still survives, the Japanese translator of the book was stabbed to death. The Italian translator was stabbed, but survived, and the Norwegian translator was shot, but lived.

COVER-UPS

A burqa is a cloak that covers up the entire body and face, with mesh in front of the eyes.

A niqab is a veil that covers the face, but leaves a space open around the eyes.

A hijab is a headscarf.

A chador is a full head-and-body cloak made from one piece of cloth that is often worn with a headscarf.

In Belgium, it is illegal to wear a burqa or full-face veil.

ISLANDS IN THE SUN

There are twenty-three thousand islands in the Pacific Ocean.

The Caribbean islands of St. Kitts and Nevis were formerly known as the Federation of St. Christopher and Nevis.

France owns a small group of islands off the east coast of Canada—St. Pierre and Miquelon.

Micronesia is north of Melanesia and west of Polynesia.

New Guinea is the second largest island in the world.

Indonesia has 130 active volcanoes, the most of any country.

Bermuda consists of 123 islands.

Bermuda is the most populous remaining British overseas territory.

The only native mammals in Bermuda are five species of bats.

CRUDE COUNTRIES

The Organization of the Petroleum Exporting Countries (OPEC) is based in Vienna, even though Austria is not a member and there are no member countries in Europe.

OPEC countries produce one-third of the world's oil.

Countries like Indonesia and Gabon had to leave OPEC when they began importing more oil than they exported.

NOTES FROM ABROAD

Iceland leads the world in births to unmarried women with 64 percent. In Italy, only 21 percent of births are to single females.

A 2003 survey found that one in fifty-five Canadian women gave birth in their cars on the way to the hospital.

Liechtenstein is the world's leading producer of sausage casings and false teeth.

Male sex offenders in the Czech Republic can volunteer to be castrated.

The Japanese keep crickets as pets.

Australia has the largest average size new house at 2,310 square feet. The United States is second at 2,169 square feet.

China and the United States are the number one and two producers of salt, respectively.

In the United Arab Emirates, 71.4 percent of the residents are foreign born.

FROM SEA TO SHINING SEA

AND BABY MAKES TWO

In 2008, 40.6 percent of U.S. births were to unwed mothers.

TIMBER!

Between 2000 and 2005, the United States lost forest cover equal in size to the state of Pennsylvania.

ON THE ROAD AGAIN

Overpasses on Interstate Highways must have at least a 16.5-foot vertical clearance (although fourteen-foot overpasses may be permissible in urban areas). This rule was established so that the system could accommodate large military apparatuses, including the atomic cannon, a scrapped weapon deployed during the Cold War. Overpasses that are too low must have on and off ramps to allow large vehicles to go around them.

Interstates are required to have at least two twelve-foot-wide lanes in each direction, a ten-foot-wide right shoulder, and a four-foot-wide left shoulder.

Those concrete barriers used to divide lanes and protect construction workers on highways are known as Jersey barriers, because they were developed for the New Jersey State Highway Department by the Stevens Institute of Technology in Hoboken, New Jersey.

I-10 in Houston is a twenty-lane highway.

SPEED DEMONS

The states in the continental United States with the fastest drivers are Mississippi, New Mexico, Idaho, Utah, and Alabama, in that order.

Delaware, Rhode Island, and Oregon have the slowest drivers.

Drivers of the Mercedes-Benz SL Class convertibles were 400 percent more likely to get a ticket than the average for American drivers of all vehicles, according to a 2010 study, the highest rate for drivers of any car. Camry Solara Coupe drivers were second at 349 percent, and Scion TC drivers were third at 343 percent.

The fastest American road is I-15 between Utah and Nevada, with posted speed limits of eighty miles per hour.

I'M, LIKE, A GOOD DRIVER

Recent research by the Allstate Foundation has found that teen girls are far more likely to talk/text/adjust music while driving. They also go more than ten miles per hour over the speed limit and drive more aggressively than teen boys. Boys were also found more likely to speak up if they were riding in a car being driven unsafely by another.

CRAWLING FROM THE WRECKAGE

Each year in the United States, about 360 people die as a result of high-speed police pursuits. One third of them are innocent victims not involved in the chase.

About 35 to 40 percent of all police chases end in a crash.

Weather causes 1.5 million car accidents a year in the United States. Snow is involved in four hundred thousand of them.

A weather phenomenon known as "tule fog" occurs in the Central Valley of California. The fog may appear suddenly and reduce visibility to near zero over vast areas. Tule fog has caused numerous multi-vehicle accidents, particularly on Highway 99, which saw a 108-car, eighteen-big-rig accident in 2007 that left two dead and thirty-nine injured and stretched for over a mile.

A 1991 dust storm near Fresno, California, resulted in five pileups involving 127 vehicles that left seventeen people dead, the most deadly weather-related accident in U.S. history.

The death rate on American roads was thirty-two times higher one hundred years ago than it is today.

Car accidents cause almost three hundred thousand traumatic brain injuries each year in the United States.

In the 1950s, fifty thousand people a year died on American roadways.

In 2009, the number of pedestrians killed by trains in the United States was 434. Trains killed 248 motorists that year.

The Fourth of July is the deadliest day on America's roadways, followed closely by January 1 and, inexplicably, August 13 and July 15.

An insurance industry study found that Rhode Island has the worst drivers in America.

BUMPER-TO-BUMPER

For every one minute that a car is disabled in a travel lane of an American highway, seven minutes of delays are caused.

It has been estimated that, each year, traffic jams cost the American economy $78 billion.

THROUGH RAIN, SLEET, AND SNOW

The first home delivery of mail in the United States started in Cleveland in 1863. The postmaster there got tired of all the people lining up at the post office awaiting mail from their loved ones off fighting the Civil War.

The advent of home delivery meant that many streets had to be named and houses needed to be assigned numbers.

The U.S. Postal Service (USPS) is the second-largest civilian employer in America. Walmart is number one.

Every one-cent increase in the price of gas costs the USPS $8 million in transportation costs.

The first postal service in the American Colonies began with a grant from William and Mary in 1692.

The first U.S. postage stamps were printed in 1847—a five-cent stamp depicting Benjamin Franklin, the first postmaster general, and a ten-cent stamp depicting George Washington. The five-cent stamp was for letters going less than three hundred miles, and the ten-cent stamp was for those going farther.

Mail was delivered seven days a week up until 1912, when religious leaders complained about mail being delivered on Sunday.

A few places, such as Loma Linda, California, get mail on Sunday. This is because the town has a large Seventh Day Adventist population that observes Saturday as their Sabbath.

Before the 1940s, residential mail was delivered at least twice a day.

Mailboxes were not required for delivery until the early 1900s.

Today, the USPS operates 32,741 post offices, which deliver to some 142 million addresses.

In 2010, the American Postal Workers Union had to postpone their internal election when their ballots got lost—in the mail.

BAD HAIR DAY

The average American woman gets about five haircuts a year.

Half of American women admit to dying their hair.

American women wash their hair an average of four times a week.

About 50 percent of American women say a bad hair day will worsen their mood.

Twenty-five percent of women say they have cried after a bad haircut.

CONTENTIOUS CAPE

Cape Canaveral, Florida, was called Cape Kennedy from 1963 to 1973. The cape had been called Canaveral for four hundred years, but when John F. Kennedy was assassinated, his wife, Jackie, asked new President Lyndon B. Johnson to rename the space center in his honor. LBJ went one better and renamed the whole cape. Residents of the city of Cape Canaveral, however, didn't go for the sudden name change, and the State of Florida restored the old name.

SAME TOWN, DIFFERENT NAME

East Detroit renamed itself Eastpointe in 1992 to remove the stigma of the word "Detroit" from its name.

A LITTLE MSG

Madison Square Park, in New York City, was named after James Madison. It is located at the intersection of Fifth Avenue and Broadway at 23rd Street. This is the site of the famous Flatiron Building.

Madison Square Garden takes its name from the square since, up until 1925, the sports arena was located nearby.

TOP NOTCHES

The little notch of land that is Erie, Pennsylvania, used to be part of New York, but was acquired by the federal government and sold to Pennsylvania in 1792 so that that state would have a port on the Great Lakes.

The notches at the southern ends of Mississippi and Alabama were acquired from Florida so that those two states, likewise, would have access to the Gulf of Mexico.

The State of Missouri has a little "boot heel" at its southeast corner. In 1818, when the boundaries of the new state were being drawn, a large landowner, John Hardeman Walker, realized that if a straight line were drawn, his land would not be in Missouri anymore, but in Arkansas. Preferring the government in Missouri, Walker greased a few palms in Washington and had the border drawn around his land, forming the boot heel.

SURVEY SAYS

Early American surveyors surveyed the entire country using metal surveying chains that were either thirty-three or sixty-six feet long.

GATEWAY TO THE WEST

The Gateway Arch in St. Louis, Missouri, is the largest chrome structure in the world.

It is 630 feet tall and is hollow, with a tram system inside that allows visitors to access an observation area at the top.

The Arch is located not far from where Lewis and Clark launched their historic expedition.

In 1980, a thrill-seeker tried to parachute onto the arch and then jump off and parachute to the ground. Unfortunately, he slid all the way down one side to his death.

GIVE ME LIBERTY

The Statue of Liberty's official name is Liberty Enlightening the World.

Sculptor Frédéric Gustav Bartholdi modeled the Statue of Liberty after his mother.

Lady Liberty's face is bigger than that of Abraham Lincoln's on Mount Rushmore.

Lady Liberty wears a size 879 shoe.

At the time of its construction, the base of the Statue of Liberty was the largest concrete structure in the United States.

It took the copper statue twenty-five years to turn blue-green, due to oxidation.

The Statue of Liberty was originally supposed to represent the goddess Isis and be dedicated at the opening of the Suez Canal in 1867. After Egypt rejected the plan, the monument was redesigned as a gift to the United States.

PRESIDENTIAL PEAK

Mount McKinley, at 20,320 feet, is the tallest mountain in North America.

It was named after Ohio native President William McKinley. A gold miner in that region of Alaska proclaimed the peak be named for McKinley, who was a strong proponent of the gold standard, in contrast to his presidential rival, William Jennings Bryan, who supported a silver standard.

Mount McKinley is often referred to by its Athabaskan Indian name—Denali ("The Great One"). Alaska officially changed the name in 1975, but the federal government has not.

Since William McKinley was from Ohio, Congressional representatives from that state have repeatedly blocked requests from the State of Alaska to change the name.

STONY FACES

Work on Mount Rushmore lasted from 1927 until 1941.

Thomas Jefferson was originally to be sculpted to the right of George Washington on Mount Rushmore, but once work was begun, it was found that the rock in this area was not suitable. The work done on Jefferson was dynamited off, and he was sculpted to the left of Washington.

Teddy Roosevelt's head is set so far back into the mountain because the rock in the originally planned location was unstable.

In 1937, a bill was introduced to Congress to add the head of Susan B. Anthony, but it never came to pass.

All four figures on Mount Rushmore were supposed to be carved down to their waists, but funds did not permit this to happen. George Washington's ascot and lapels were carved before this change in plans.

The memorial has only been cleaned once in its history. That was in 2005.

HEAD COUNT

The U.S. Constitution mandates a census be taken every ten years to apportion seats in the House of Representatives.

The first U.S. Census was taken in 1790.

Individual census records are sealed for seventy-two years to ensure confidentiality.

Census privacy laws are to help encourage illegal immigrants and those hiding from the government to fill out the form. President Franklin Delano Roosevelt broke this rule when he used Census data to round up Japanese-Americans during World War II.

In 2010, the U.S. Census Bureau hired seven hundred thousand temporary employees to go to every address where a Census form was not filled out, to get the information.

BLUE BALL AND BIG BEAVER

Pennsylvania may have the greatest number of strange place-names of any state, such as:

Analomink

Balls Mills

Bastress

Big Beaver

Blue Ball

Butztown

Climax

Fertility

Jugtown

Lickdale

Ogle

Stalker

Virginville

. . . and, of course, the ever popular Intercourse, Pennsylvania.

PERVS

There are seven hundred thousand sex offenders in the United States.

The average jail time for child sex offenders in the United States is three years.

GONE MISSING

Of the 840,279 missing person cases in 2001, almost eight hundred thousand of these were minors. "Only" about one hundred are children abducted by strangers. The vast majority of missing juveniles are runaways or were taken by family members involved in custody disputes.

GENERAL HEALTH

The post of surgeon general was created as the officer in charge of the Marine Hospital Service in 1871. The quasi-military service was formed to fight the spread of diseases by merchant sailors.

Today, the service is called the Public Health Service Commissioned Corps and is one of only seven uniformed services in the U.S. government.

Surgeons general hold the rank of vice admiral in the Corps.

STRAPHANGERS

The New York City Subway system is the only one in the world that operates twenty-four hours a day, seven days a week, 365 days a year.

Five million passengers ride NYC subways every weekday.

Enterprising scammers used to jam paper into the token slots on the turnstiles and literally suck out deposited tokens using their mouths.

DAMMING INFO

Hoover Dam construction began under the Hoover administration in 1930, but Franklin Delano Roosevelt was elected before it was completed and had the name changed to Boulder Dam. In 1947, Harry S. Truman restored Hoover's name to the dam.

The concrete for Hoover Dam had to be poured and cooled in layers, because concrete contracts and heats up as it cures. If it had been done in one huge block, the concrete would have taken 125 years to cool to ambient temperature. The concrete is still curing and gaining strength today.

Hoover Dam's builders used enough concrete to pave a two-lane highway from New York to San Francisco.

Ninety-six workers died during the construction of Hoover Dam.

Grand Coulee Dam in Washington State is the largest concrete structure in the country and the largest electric-power-producing facility.

THE JURY IS IN

In many places in the United States, a grand jury decides whether there is enough evidence for a case to go to trial. It is comprised of many more jurors than a petit (trial) jury of twelve.

The United States is the only country that still uses grand juries.

Only half of the states employ grand juries; the rest use preliminary hearings before a judge to evaluate evidence and recommend whether a prosecution should proceed.

Studies have found that unattractive defendants are more likely to be convicted and receive sentences twenty-two months longer than good-looking ones.

American judges set aside (overrule) only one-half of one percent of jury verdicts.

IT SURE FEELS LIKE
WE'RE MARRIED

Common-law marriage is valid in fourteen states—
Alabama, Colorado, Georgia, Idaho (only if before January 1, 1996), Iowa, Kansas, Montana, North Carolina,
Ohio (only if before October 10, 1991), Oklahoma,
Pennsylvania (only if before January 1, 2005), Rhode Island, South Carolina, Texas, and Washington, DC.

The IRS does not recognize common-law marriage.

FALL GUYS

Niagara Falls is only 12,300 years old.

> Sixteen people have taken the plunge over Niagara
> Falls.

In 1918, a barge working upstream of the falls broke
free of its tow and nearly went over the edge before the
crew managed to ground it on some rocks just at the
precipice.

> The greatest distance anyone has ever fallen without
> a parachute and survived is thirty-three thousand
> feet.

In 2010, a New York City man survived a thirty-nine
story fall in which he crashed through the rear window
of a parked car.

RED LAKE, BLUE LAKE

The Great Salt Lake in Utah is divided by a railroad causeway. The water north of the causeway is much more salty than the water on the south side. As a result, the upper portion is a wine red color due to the red algae and bacteria that grow there, and the lower portion is bluish water due to the blue-green algae that thrive there. Viewed from above, the causeway makes a perfectly straight line dividing the red and blue halves.

THE MOTHER OF ALL HOLES

The Bingham Canyon Mine in Utah is the largest and deepest open-pit mine in the world, at 2.5 miles wide with a depth of 0.75 miles. It is so big that it is visible from outer space.

The mine has yielded more copper than any in the world, except the Chuquicamata Mine in Chile.

The value of the ore extracted from the Bingham Canyon Mine (more than 17 million tons of copper) is greater than that of the California Gold Rush, Comstock Lode, and Klondike Gold Rush combined. In 2006 alone, the mine produced $1.8 billion in metals.

Every day, 450,000 tons of material is removed from the mine by huge dump trucks costing $3 million each.

TAXING READING

The instruction booklet for filling out the 1040 tax form was just two pages in 1935. By 2009, it had swollen to 172 pages.

Only 47 percent of Americans paid federal income taxes in 2009.

Fifty percent of tax-paying Americans hire a professional to do their taxes.

The Internal Revenue Service will go back no more than three years on a normal audit. They will go back six years if income is underreported by 25 percent or more, and can go back an unlimited number of years if no return is filed or if a fraudulent return is filed.

YOU

The average American born today will live about seventy-eight years.

In that time, he or she will consume the equivalent of 13,000 pints of milk, 1,400 chickens, 19,800 eggs, 14,000 candy bars, 4,400 loaves of bread, 20,000 potatoes, and 43,000 cans of soda.

The average American will have used almost 2 million gallons of water in their lifetime. This is equivalent to letting the faucet run for two years.

Each American generates fifteen tons of trash during his or her lifetime.

The energy required to support one American throughout his or her life is the equivalent of 285 tons of coal.

Thirty-one percent of American women ages fifteen to forty-four are on the pill, 27 percent have had tubal ligations, 18 percent make their partners use condoms, and 9 percent have partners who have had a vasectomy.

The average American baby will go through 3,800 diapers. To make that many diapers will require 1,900 pints of crude oil, 715 pounds of plastic, and four and a half trees.

UNITED STATES

America consumes 1.6 billion pounds of food a day.

Americans eat 47 billion hamburgers a year.

On the Fourth of July, Americans down 150 million hot dogs. If that many wieners were lined up end to end, they would stretch the length of the entire coastline of the United States.

American hens lay 76 billion eggs each year.

Americans spend more on beauty aids than on education.

TEXAS TEA

The first major Texas oil well—Spindletop—was drilled in 1901, resulting in an oil boom.

Texas oil production peaked in 1972.

The United States is the number three producer of petroleum, behind number one Russia and number two Saudi Arabia.

No new oil refineries have been built in the United States since 1976.

FIVE AND DIME

The dollar sign ($) does not appear on any U.S. currency.

The 1909 Lincoln penny was the first American coin to depict a president.

Between 1943 and 1946, pennies were made of zinc-coated steel, saving enough copper for the war effort to make 1.25 million ammunition shells.

The U.S. Mint in Philadelphia can make one million pennies in forty-five minutes.

Some states and local governments used to make one-tenth cent pieces out of tin, aluminum, plastic, and paper.

The original American "nickel" was the 1859 copper-nickel Indian cent. In 1865, a three-cent coin was designated the "nickel." It wasn't until 1866 that the five cent shield nickel was introduced, and U.S. five-cent pieces have been called nickels ever since.

In 2007, the value of the nickel and copper found in a nickel was about nine cents. To curtail entrepreneurs from melting down nickels for their metal content, the U.S. Mint made it illegal to do so. As of 2009, the metal found in a nickel is worth less than five cents, so this is no longer an issue.

Dimes are so small because prior to 1965 they had a 90 percent silver content. If they were any larger, their intrinsic value would have exceeded their face value.

The 1916–1945 dimes, commonly known as "Mercury heads," do not in fact depict the god Mercury, but the mythological goddess Liberty.

In 1946, shortly after FDR's death, his image replaced Liberty's on the dime. Part of the reasoning for this was that FDR had helped to found the organization that had become the March of Dimes.

The FDR dime was designed by the chief engraver at the U.S. Mint—John Sinnock—who put his initials at the bottom of Roosevelt's neck. Rumors flew that the letters

"JS" stood for Joseph Stalin and had been put there by a communist at the mint.

DOES ANYBODY REALLY KNOW WHAT TIME IT IS?

Before 1883, there were eight thousand different times zones in the United States. (Each town set its time by the sun.)

BRASS CASTLE

The Pentagon is the largest office building in the world, based on floor space. It has seventeen and a half miles of hallways and is so big that it has been assigned six different zip codes.

> More than two hundred thousand phone calls and one million emails are sent and received each day at the Pentagon.

There are 4,200 clocks in the Pentagon.

> The Pentagon employs twenty-three thousand people.

The windows in the Pentagon, which do not open, weigh almost one ton each and have glass panes two inches thick.

> The Pentagon got its shape because of the position of the roads that surrounded the original building site—they formed a pentagon.

The terrorist attack on September 11, 2001, occurred exactly sixty years to the day after the Pentagon's groundbreaking.

SAY WHAT?

The capital of South Dakota is Pierre, pronounced *peer*.

Newark, Delaware, is pronounced *nu ark*; whereas Newark, New Jersey, is pronounced *nu erk*.

SCIENCE PROJECT

OUT OF THIS WORLD

Ten different countries have the ability to launch satellites into space for their own use and for other nations.

More than fifty nations have satellites in space.

The European Space Agency (ESA) launches missions from its spaceport in French Guiana in South America. Since the spaceport is only 310 miles north of the equator, the earth's rotation adds 1,100 miles per hour to a rocket's trajectory when launched toward the east. The Canadian Space Agency is a cooperating member of the ESA.

In 1957, the first American attempt to launch a satellite into space ended in failure when the rocket carrying it exploded four feet off the ground.

SPACE JUNK

There is so much space debris in low earth orbit that there is a danger of something known as the Kessler syndrome, where two objects collide and create much more space debris, which strikes more objects, creating a chain reaction of debris and collisions that eventually destroys all the satellites in that orbit.

To help avoid the possibility of Kessler syndrome, many defunct satellites are boosted into a higher orbit, known as a "graveyard" orbit, to keep them safely out of the way of lower-orbit functional satellites.

Soviet military and spy satellites of the 1970s were powered with nuclear reactors. Most were boosted to graveyard orbits after they became nonoperational. However, many malfunctioned and remained in lower orbits. Two have crashed to earth with their radioactive material intact. One spread debris across northern Canada in 1978, and another fell into the Indian Ocean in 1983.

In 2009, the first collision of two satellites occurred. An out-of-service Russian Space Forces satellite struck an operating U.S. communications satellite at more than 27,000 miles per hour.

Some of the more interesting space debris includes a glove lost by American astronaut Ed White on the first ever space walk, along with a tool bag, a pair of pliers, a camera, and a toothbrush lost on other space walks.

A 2007 Chinese anti-satellite-missile test created thousands of pieces of dangerous debris in the most densely populated orbit.

The U.S. Space Surveillance Network currently tracks eight thousand pieces of space debris that may be of concern.

In 1997, a woman in Oklahoma was hit by a piece of falling debris from a U.S. Air Force Delta II rocket that had been launched a year earlier. Happily, she was not injured.

UNIVERSAL TRUTHS

The universe looks the same in every direction, as observed from the earth.

According to theoretical physicists, during the Big Bang, the universe expanded from an infinitely dense speck the size of an atom to the size of a baseball in a millionth of a millionth of a millionth of a millionth of a second. That's the equivalent of going from the size of a golf ball to the size of Earth.

Cosmologists also believe that at the moment of the Big Bang there were a billion and one particles of matter for every billion particles of antimatter. Each antimatter particle destroyed a particle of matter. The remaining particles of matter are what make up everything in the universe today.

Three minutes after the Big Bang, only the elements hydrogen, helium, lithium, and beryllium existed, and only as atomic nuclei. It took another three hundred thousand years for things to cool down enough to form actual atoms.

It is thought that only 4 percent of the universe is made up of ordinary matter. The rest is believed to be dark energy and dark matter.

Super-massive black holes can be four billion times as massive as the sun.

The crust of a neutron star is 10 billion times stronger than steel.

The rotation period of a neutron star is so precisely regular that it is more accurate than an atomic clock.

GALAXY QUEST

The Milky Way galaxy is hurtling through space toward its closest neighbor—the Andromeda galaxy—at one million miles per hour. In less than four billion years, the two will collide.

The Milky Way is not very crowded. There are approximately 30 trillion miles between stars.

It takes the sun 300 million years to make one complete circle around the Milky Way galaxy.

There are estimated to be about 170 billion galaxies in the observable universe.

SUNNY AND HOT

The sun's surface temperature is 10,000°F. Its corona, or atmosphere, is two hundred times hotter.

Three percent of the sun's energy is in the form of neutrinos. Neutrinos are minuscule, electrically neutral particles produced by nuclear fusion. They are so small that they can pass right through the earth (and you) unimpeded.

Each second, 65 billion neutrinos made by the sun pass through each cubic centimeter of the earth.

SPACE WEATHER

Solar storms are events on the sun that cause solar flares and coronal mass ejections (CMEs). A CME is a plasma burst of electrons and protons that bombards the earth.

The solar storm of 1859 knocked out telegraph service around the world. Because of this solar storm, brilliant auroras, or northern lights (natural light displays caused by the interaction of the earth's magnetic field with the solar wind), occurred as far south as the Caribbean. Solar storms on this scale are believed to happen once every five hundred years or so.

If such a storm were to occur today, all satellites would be knocked out, as well as much of the electronics and power grids on earth, bringing modern society to a grinding halt.

In 1989, a massive solar flare knocked out the power grid to the entire province of Quebec.

Green-colored auroras are caused by oxygen atoms in the upper atmosphere that are excited by the solar wind. Blue and red auroras are caused by nitrogen atoms.

Auroras make sounds that can be heard by people on the ground.

3RD ROCK FROM THE SUN

The inner core of the earth is made of solid iron and nickel. The inner core's extreme pressure prevents the metals from melting. The outer core, however, is comprised of liquid metals, which give the earth its magnetic fields.

The earth bulges at the equator because of its rotation.

Earth's rotation is slowing at a rate of 1.7 seconds per year, meaning 350 million years ago, the length of an earth year was 400 to 410 days.

Seven hundred million years ago, the surface of the earth was frozen solid, with the oceans covered in ice one mile thick.

APOCALYPSE NOW?

There is about one million square miles of space between each asteroid in the asteroid belt, which lies between the orbits of Mars and Jupiter.

If all the asteroids in the belt were grouped together, they would form a body about one-half the size of the moon.

Some asteroids are composed of up to 98 percent iron.

A meteorite hits Earth at forty thousand miles per hour, or twenty times faster than a bullet.

A "keyhole" is a very small area of space where Earth's gravity is slightly stronger than elsewhere.

If an asteroid were to pass through a keyhole, the slight disturbance in its course could cause it to hit Earth on its next orbital pass. This is the case with the 1,300-foot asteroid known as Apophis that will pass close to Earth in 2029. There is a two-thousand-foot diameter keyhole that may be in the path of Apophis, which could alter its path, causing it to strike Earth in 2036.

Each day, about forty tons of sand-to-dust-sized particles of space debris rain down on Earth.

THE BIG CHILL

North America and Europe experienced prolonged periods of intermittent cool weather from the sixteenth century to the nineteenth century, known as the Little Ice Age.

In the mid-1600s, the Baltic Sea froze over, allowing people to walk from Poland to Sweden across the ice.

In the winter of 1607, ice remained on Lake Superior until June.

During the winter of 1780, New York Harbor froze over, allowing people to walk from Manhattan to Staten Island.

Cold weather forced winegrowing in Northern Europe to move to Southern Europe over the centuries. Early England had a flourishing viticulture, but by 1440, it had virtually disappeared due to much cooler temperatures.

The colder, shorter growing seasons in Northern Europe caused tree rings to become much closer together, circa 1645 to 1750, resulting in denser wood. It is the dense wood of this time that is credited with giving Antonio Stradivari's violins their unique sound.

INCONVENIENT TRUTHS

Contrary to popular myth, Antarctica as a whole is getting cooler, not warmer. While ice in areas of western Antarctica is melting, this is more than offset by the cooling and expansion of ice on the eastern side of the continent.

The melting of sea ice does not raise the water levels of the oceans, since the water (ice) is already in the ocean. Only melting ice sheets and polar cap ice over land can raise sea levels.

Before the protective ozone layer formed 300 million years ago, life could not emerge from the oceans without being fried.

JOURNEY TO THE CENTER OF THE EARTH

The deepest hole ever drilled is the Kola Superdeep Borehole in Russia. It goes down 40,230 feet into the ground, roughly one-third of the way through the earth's mantle.

It is not possible to drill much deeper than this because at that depth the temperature is too high for drill bits to properly function.

At forty-nine thousand feet, temperatures reach 570°F.

DRIFTING AWAY

Due to continental drift, North America and Europe move one inch farther from each other each year.

WHICHEVER WAY
THE WIND BLOWS

Think a gust of wind is just a gust of wind? Think again. There are many categories of winds recognized in North America. Here's a list of several:

Alberta clipper: a small cyclonic storm in the Rocky Mountains of Alberta, Canada, that moves southeast into the Great Plains, where it is followed by cold polar air

Backing wind: a wind that shifts counterclockwise

Black blizzard, or black roller: a severe dust storm that darkens the sky over the Great Plains

Blue norther: an outbreak of cold air in Texas that produces a dark, blue-black sky

Boulder wind: a strong downslope wind in the Front Range near Boulder, Colorado

Cow-killer: strong east to northeast winds coming down from the mountains in Washington State

Newhall winds: downslope winds blowing from the desert uplands through Newhall Pass into California's San Fernando Valley

Palousers: dangerous winds in the Palouser River valley in northern Idaho and eastern Washington

Plow, or plough, winds: straight-line winds, associated with thunderstorms, that blow in the Midwest

Santa Ana: hot, dry, gusty winds that blow from the upland deserts of Southern California down to the coastal plain

Sea turn: cool, moist easterly winds that blow off the coast of New England, producing fog and drizzle

Siberian express: strong, cold cyclonic winds that blow from Alaska, through Canada, and into the lower forty-eight states

Sonora: a wind that blows from Sonora, Mexico, into Southern California

Texas norther: strong north flow winds on the southern plains that can lower the temperature up to thirty degrees in just a few minutes

Wasatch winds: very strong easterly winds that blow out of canyon mouths in the Wasatch Valley in Utah and may reach hurricane force

Washoe zephyr: westerly winds that blow down the eastern side of the Sierra Nevada Mountains

SNOW JOB

A snow tremor, or snow quake, occurs when a large field of snow settles down on an air pocket beneath it, producing a very loud sound.

A snow geyser can result during a snow quake, as snow may be blown up into the air from a crack in the collapsing snow pack.

WHAT THE HAIL?

A falling icy conglomeration officially becomes a hailstone when the ice pellet reaches one-fifth of an inch in diameter. Smaller ice pellets are known as sleet.

A hailshaft is a column of hail falling from a single thunderstorm cell.

A hailstreak is the hail dropped by a hailshaft as it sweeps along the ground.

The largest hailstone reliably reported in the United States fell in Vivian, South Dakota, in 2010 and measured about eight inches in diameter with a weight of almost two pounds.

Large hailstones can fall to Earth at upwards of one hundred miles per hour.

One severe hailstorm that hit Selden, Kansas, in 1959 dumped up to eighteen inches of hail on the ground.

"Hail Alley," the High Plains region east of the Rocky Mountains, receives the most hailstorms in North America.

Cheyenne, Wyoming, is the most hail-prone city in North America, getting about ten hailstorms a year.

The Pacific Coast is the region of the continental United States to receive the fewest hailstorms.

One 1888 hailstorm reported in northern India is believed to have killed 246 people and 1,600 goats.

Fourteen people were killed in a 2007 hailstorm in China.

The most recently confirmed hailstorm death in the United States was that of an infant killed while held in its mother's arms, in Fort Collins, Colorado, in 1979.

COOL DOWN

Nuclear fuel rods used in nuclear reactors are used for five years. Then they get deposited into pools of water to cool down, which may take up to twenty years.

MELT DOWN

It took five hundred thousand workers to put out the fire and clean up the debris after the 1986 Chernobyl nuclear reactor meltdown.

Twenty thousand firefighters died from radiation poisoning and another two hundred thousand became permanently disabled.

Today, wildlife in the seventeen-mile exclusion zone set up around Chernobyl has flourished due to the absence of humans. Many endangered species thrive there, and the plant growth is lush. The area has been turned into a wildlife sanctuary.

Due to radioactive fallout that still contaminates the soil in Germany, many of the wild boars there are radioactive, which is a problem because boar meat is considered a delicacy by many. The fungi that the boars feed on accumulate the radioactivity as they grow in the dirt.

BETTER LIVING THROUGH CHEMISTRY

There are more than 30 million known chemical substances.

Each year, four hundred thousand new substances are described in science journals.

A substance known as hafnium carbide has the highest melting point known—7,520°F.

The term "pH" stands for "potential of hydrogen."

ALL WET

The hydrogen atoms in all the water in the universe were created in the Big Bang.

Water is the only non-metallic substance that expands when it freezes.

Ice floats because its crystalline structure has a lot of empty spaces, making it lighter than liquid water.

There are fifteen different ice phases (crystalline structures of ice) that can be formed at varying temperatures and pressures.

Researchers believe that there is more water to be found *under* the oceans than is contained *in* the oceans.

The size of a swimming pool used in the Olympics is fifty meters long. It is unlikely many homes have such a large pool.

The Great Lakes system is the largest body of freshwater on the planet.

It takes 528 gallons of water to make one T-shirt.

Nine billion gallons of bottled water are sold every year in the United States. That's 50 billion bottles.

COLD HARD FACTS

The generally accepted reason for why ice is slippery is that the molecules on the outermost layer that are in contact with the air do not properly bond with the molecules below. This means they are in a semiliquid state and are free to easily move, acting as a lubricant.

During the first nonstop flight across the Atlantic, in 1919, ice formed on the wings of the airplane. British pilot Arthur Whitten Brown had to crawl out on the wings several times during the flight to dislodge ice.

IT'S ELEMENTARY

The most expensive element is rhodium, which is used in airplane spark plugs and jewelry. It goes for $2,500 an ounce.

The elements astatine and protactinium are the rarest on Earth. There is less than one ounce of astatine in the entire world.

The newest element, discovered in Russia in 2010, is called ununseptium. Only six atoms of the stuff have been created.

SALT OF THE EARTH

The two elemental components of salt, sodium (Na) and chlorine (Cl), are both very nasty elements on their own. Sodium is a highly reactive metal that will burst into flames and explode when added to water. Chlorine gas was used as a weapon during World War I and was responsible for ninety-one thousand deaths.

Salt lowers the freezing point of water to zero degrees Fahrenheit.

HEAVY METAL

All the heavy metals on Earth, including silver and gold, were created by supernova explosions billions of years ago.

Two-thirds of the elements on the periodic table are metals.

It has been estimated that it will take forty-five thousand pounds of metal to sustain each individual who was born in 2006 over his or her lifetime.

COMPLETELY COPPER

The symbol for copper is Cu, which is from the Latin *cuprum*. The Roman's supply of the metal came from Cyprus, and they called it *aes cyprium*, later shortened to *cyprium* and then corrupted to *cuprum*, and then to "copper" in English.

The average home contains about four hundred pounds of copper.

Copper has a germicidal effect.

Brass doorknobs naturally disinfect themselves within eight hours of being touched. For this reason, brass, or copper-coated doorknobs are use in many hospitals.

Silver also kills germs. Water tanks on ships and planes are often silvered. Silverware, likewise, self-sterilizes.

DENSE AND DEADLY

Uranium is named for the planet Uranus, which was discovered eight years before the element.

Uranium is the second densest naturally occurring element, after plutonium.

One-half of the uranium used to fuel U.S. nuclear power plants comes from dismantled Soviet/Russian warheads.

The atomic bomb that destroyed Hiroshima used uranium. The one dropped on Nagasaki relied on plutonium.

The amount of matter converted to energy in the Hiroshima bomb was less than the mass in one-third of a dime.

Uranium is only naturally formed in supernovas.

NOTHIN' BUT NICKEL

The element nickel got its name from medieval German miners who attempted to extract copper from a red mineral they had found but were unable to do so. They blamed this on the mischievous sprite of German mythology—Nickel.

Most of the world's nickel comes from the site of a huge meteor strike in Ontario and a large deposit in Russia.

Coltan, short for Columbite-tantalite, is a dull, metallic ore. When refined, it yields tantalum, a heat-resistant powder that can hold a charge and is essential in cell phones, laptops, and video game systems.

SILENT SPRING

DDT (dichlorodiphenyltrichloroethane) was first synthesized in 1874 by Austrian chemist Othmar Zeidler, who couldn't find a use for it. Its potential for killing insects was not realized until 1939.

In 1948, Swiss chemist Paul Hermann Müller was awarded the Nobel Prize in Physiology or Medicine for discovering the insecticidal properties of DDT.

DDT was banned in America in 1972, because many argued that the reduction in certain bird populations was due to the thinning of eggshells thought to be caused by DDT.

Rachel Carson's 1962 book, *Silent Spring*, served as the impetus to ban DDT and is credited with launching the environmental movement.

Many other countries continued to use DDT and U.S. manufacturers happily supplied their needs.

SHOCKINGLY ECCENTRIC

Nikola Tesla is the scientist primarily responsible for the widespread use of alternating current. Alternating current (AC) differs from direct current (DC) in that, in AC, the electric charge periodically changes direction while, in DC, it continuously flows in one direction. Tesla also invented the electric motor and the automotive ignition system.

Tesla never married, was obsessed with pigeons, and actually considered one to be his "wife."

Tesla had an irrational compulsion involving the number three. His hotel room numbers had to be divisible by three. He insisted on having nine napkins and nine slices of bread sent to his room.

Tesla was disgusted by overweight people, pierced ears, and pearl earrings.

The eccentric genius believed that he had received communications from outer space.

He went to work for Thomas Edison, who stiffed him out of a fifty-thousand-dollar bonus. As payback, Tesla left Edison's lab and went on to promote the widespread use of AC current, dashing Edison's obsession with making his DC current the preferred current.

Guglielmo Marconi, who is often credited with inventing the radio, used seventeen of Tesla's patents in the process. The Supreme Court ruled in 1943 that the patent rights for the radio belonged to Tesla, not Marconi.

EN "LIGHT" ENMENT

According to the Big Bang theory, it took five hundred thousand years for the early universe to expand enough for light particles to travel freely, i.e., produce light.

A beam of light would circle the earth seven times in one second.

It takes light one hundred thousand years to travel across the Milky Way galaxy.

Light travels 5,900 billion miles in one year. This distance is known as a light year.

The shortest length of time that has been measured is called an attosecond—one quintillionth of a second, or the time it takes light to travel the length of three hydrogen atoms. To put that into perspective, one attosecond is to one second what one second is to the age of the universe (about 13.7 billion years).

According to Albert Einstein, nothing can go faster than the speed of light, except the expansion of the universe.

Diamonds sparkle because the tight carbon atom matrices they are made of slow down light particles, which bounce this way and that to find a way out, producing the sparkle.

Lenses bend light by causing it to slow down.

A big gherkin pickle will glow like a bright yellow light-bulb if it is put between two electrical leads plugged into a wall outlet. (But don't try this at home!)

Incandescent lightbulbs are filled with argon gas.

Ninety percent of the energy used to light an incandescent bulb is lost as heat. Only 10 percent comes out as light.

On the vernal equinox—March 20—night and day are the same length of time around the globe.

Ninety percent of deep ocean life is bioluminescent.

Navy pilots used to find their aircraft carriers at night by following the bioluminescent trail left in the ship's wake.

TUNING IN

In 1912, it was decided that each country would be assigned letters to identify radio stations. The United States was assigned "K" and "W" to begin radio call letters. In 1924, the Federal Communications Commission ruled that new stations east of the Mississippi would start with "W" and those to the west would use "K."

Canadian radio stations begin with a "C" and Mexican stations with an "X."

MERCHANT OF DEATH

Nitroglycerine was invented by Italian chemist Ascanio Sobrero, in 1847.

When nitroglycerin explodes it produces heat of 9000°F.

Alfred Nobel, an armaments manufacturer, began manufacturing liquid nitroglycerine in the 1860s with some disregard for its volatility. His brother Emil was killed by a blast at their armaments factory, and several other catastrophes occurred while transporting the stuff.

To make it safer to handle, Nobel mixed nitroglycerine with powdered diatomaceous earth, and dynamite was created.

Originally, Nobel had wanted to name his invention "Nobel's Safety Powder," but settled on "dynamite," after the Greek word for "power."

When his brother Ludvig died in 1888, a French newspaper mistakenly published an obituary for Alfred that called him "the merchant of death." This so upset Nobel that he changed his will to leave the bulk of his estate (about $250 million in today's money) to create the Nobel prizes.

There is no Nobel Prize in mathematics because Alfred Nobel considered mathematics to be an "auxiliary" science.

Nobel's father, Immanuel, invented plywood.

PRICE CHECK

A Uniform Price Code (UPC) bar code is a series of fifty-nine alternating black and white lines of varying widths. These lines correspond to twelve numerals when read by an optical scanner. These are the twelve numbers that appear below the code.

Each of the twelve numbers is represented by four lines—two white and two black. There are also three lines at each end of the code and five in the middle that act as standards.

The first six numerals represent the manufacturer of the product. The next five stand for the manufacturer's product number, and the last digit is a check digit, which must match a mathematical calculation done by the scanner using the first eleven numbers. A mismatch needs to be rescanned.

Price is not included on a UPC bar code. This is stored in the retailer's main computer. The scanner tells the computer the product and the computer sends back the price.

Store bonus cards and gift cards have more digits than UPCs.

Store "bonus" or "reward" cards allow the retailer to track what someone buys. Retailers have been known to contact police when they perceive "suspicious" buying patterns. One Pennsylvania man was arrested by police after the supermarket he frequented noticed that he was buying a lot of wooden matches. Police obtained a search warrant and found a meth lab at his home. (The red phosphorous in the match heads is used to make meth.)

LITTER, LITTER EVERYWHERE

Between 60 and 80 percent of the garbage in the oceans originated as litter on land.

A recent survey found that, numberwise, cigarette butts are the most prevalent type of litter on American beaches and intercoastal waterways, followed by plastic bags, food wrappers, caps and lids, and plastic bottles.

FOOLING AROUND WITH FOOD

A gene gun is a device that blasts tiny bits of DNA-covered gold into plant or animal cells to add specific desired genes to an organism. In plants, this type of genetic engineering allows plant breeders to add genes from one species to another, usually genes for resistance to certain diseases or drought tolerance.

Approximately 80 percent of the corn, cotton, and soybeans grown in the United States are genetically engineered crops.

Scientists have genetically engineered corn plants to release a chemical into the soil when attacked by rootworms that will "call" parasitic roundworms from the surrounding soil to attack and kill the rootworms.

GONE IN A FLASH

North America receives the most lightning strikes of any continent. Around the world there are 8 million lightning strikes per day.

The United States receives some 20 million strikes a year.

Rwanda has the most lightning strikes per square mile.

People in Florida are thirty-four times more likely to be struck by lightning than the average American. Between 2000 and 2009, seventy people in Florida were killed by lightning. During the same time period, no one in Alaska, Hawaii, Delaware, New Hampshire, North Dakota, Oregon, Washington State, or Washington, DC, was killed by lightning.

Half of the people who are struck by lightning survive.

The energy in a bolt of lightning is less than that in a liter of heating oil.

Volcanic ash clouds and forest fires can produce lightning, as the dust they create causes static charges in the air.

Lightning is hot enough to fuse silica sand in the ground and form glass.

Benjamin Franklin's key-on-the-kite-string lightning experiment in 1752 was not the first. A French experimenter had tried the same test a few weeks earlier than Franklin.

Franklin did not hold the kite string, but tied it to a post to observe what would happen.

In subsequent years, there were many fatalities of those trying to replicate Franklin's experiment.

The typical lightning strike is composed of a series of several strokes and restrokes.

Elms and oaks are the trees most frequently struck by lightning.

Bark blows off trees when they are hit because the heat causes the sap to boil violently under pressure and explode.

The Empire State Building is struck by lightning an average of twenty-three times a year. It was once struck eight times in twenty-four minutes.

When lightning strikes near a compass, the needle spins wildly, due to the electromagnetic field that is generated.

Lightning produces X-rays.

The fear of lightning is called astraphobia.

WITH A TWIST

Tornadoes in the Northern Hemisphere usually rotate counterclockwise. One in a hundred rotate clockwise.

The average tornado stays on the ground ten minutes.

The Tri-State Tornado, which tore through Missouri, Illinois, and Indiana on March 18, 1925, had a path 219 miles in length, a speed of 73 mph, and lasted three and a half hours, all records.

MEDICAL CENTER

BUBBLE BOY

David Vetter is better known as the "Bubble Boy." Ten seconds after he was born in 1972, David was put into a sterile, plastic cocoon. Anything that entered the "bubble" had to be sterilized, and he could only interact with other people through rubber gloves in the side of the "bubble." When David was six, NASA made him a special fifty-thousand-dollar space suit to wear outside the bubble, but he only used it a few times. The suit is now in the Smithsonian Institute.

The only time David ever got sick was when he received a bone marrow transplant from his sister in 1984. He died two weeks later.

After his death, his parents divorced, and his mother married a *People* magazine reporter who had covered the story.

BODY OF KNOWLEDGE

The brain makes one hundred trillion calculations per second.

The body is constantly replacing old cells. In ten years' time, a whole new body will have been created.

The only parts of the body that do not make new cells are the inner lenses of the eyes, the heart, and parts of the brain. These body parts will have the same cells at age eighty as they did at age one.

The skin produces thirty thousand new cells every minute.

Hair is modified dead skin cells.

The body grows seven miles of hair per year. (This includes all body hair.)

There really are six senses—taste, touch, sight, hearing, smell, *and* balance.

While the brain only comprises about 2 percent of one's total body weight, it requires 20 percent of the body's blood volume.

At the time of death, hearing is the last sense to go.

CHEW ON THIS

The small intestine has so many microscopic folds that its total surface area would measure 2,800 square feet if stretched out.

The body digests carbohydrates much faster than fats. Carbs will be digested within twenty-four hours, proteins within forty-eight hours, and fats take up to seventy-two hours.

Alcohol and protein take the most energy to digest.

While the tryptophan found in turkey can cause drowsiness, the proteins in the meat largely negate this effect.

Most of the mood-altering hormone in the body is produced in the stomach lining.

The stomach cannot digest hair or chewing gum.

SEEING DOUBLE

There are roughly 50 million pairs of twins worldwide.

Heteropaternal superfecundation refers to twins from separate fathers. This can result when a woman releases multiple eggs in a single cycle and has sex with more than one man.

Half identical, or polar body twins, are very similar, but do not share 100 percent of each other's DNA. Scientists aren't sure exactly how this happens.

Mirror image twins are identical twins who share traits in a reverse symmetry, as if looking at each other in a mirror. They may have birthmarks or cowlicks on opposite sides. One may be left-handed and one right-handed. This type of twinning occurs when the fertilized egg splits late in the embryonic development.

Identical twins have different fingerprints.

THANKS, MOM

A nursing mother absorbs germs from her baby through her breasts to which her body makes antibodies that she gives back to the baby through her milk.

Fetuses yawn.

A two-year-old learns about ten new words a day.

In the United States, 32 percent of babies are delivered through cesarean sections. Half of the babies in China are delivered this way.

A C-section is the most common surgery performed in America after circumcision.

MEDICALLY SPEAKING

The following are the medical terms for some rather mundane things:

Sphenopalatineganglioneuralgia is better known as brain freeze.

Otitis externa is swimmer's ear.

Borborygmi is stomach growling.

Emesis is vomiting.

Pandiculation is yawning.

Sternulation is sneezing.

Stertor is snoring.

IT'S MORE FUN TO WATCH

Sexologist Alfred Kinsey started out studying gall wasps at Harvard, where he earned his PhD, and began studying human sexuality while a professor at Indiana University.

Kinsey encouraged his graduate students, wife, and staff to engage in group sex. He included in his research secret interviews of active pedophile men who recounted their experiences with children.

Kinsey and his research assistants William Howell Masters and Virginia Eshelman Johnson began filming people having sex and masturbating in 1957. They also hooked them up to polygraph-like instruments to measure their sexual response. The culmination of their sexual observations was the 1966 bestselling book *Human Sexual Response*. In it, they defined four sexual stages— excitement, plateau, orgasm, and resolution.

The researchers also assigned homosexual men and lesbian women random partners and observed. From 1968 until 1977, they tried to convert homosexuals into heterosexuals.

Apparently, all the watching of others doing it must have also stimulated the researchers. Masters dumped his wife and married Johnson in 1971.

SCAN THIS

Antimatter is used during a PET (positron emission tomography) scan. Positrons, which are anti-electrons, are introduced into the human tissue being scanned. When they meet electrons, the two annihilate each other, producing gamma photons that are detected by the scanner and used to form a three-dimensional picture of the tissue.

CAT scan is short for computerized axial tomography.

PHOBIA FEST

Some people suffer from odd fears, such as:

Ablutophobia: the fear of bathing

Apeirophobia: the fear of infinity

Automatonophobia: the fear of ventriloquists' dummies

Barophobia: the fear of gravity

Basophobia: the fear of walking

Caligynephobia: the fear of beautiful women

Chrometophobia: the fear of money

Cibophobia: the fear of food

Consecotaleophobia: the fear of chopsticks

Ephebiphobia: the fear of teenagers

Geliophobia: the fear of laughter or smiling

Geniophobia: the fear of chins

Genuphobia: the fear of knees

Hexakosioihexekontahexaphobia: the fear of the number 666

Kathisophobia: the fear of sitting down

Medomalacuphobia: the fear of losing an erection

Neophobia: the fear of anything new

Omphalophobia: the fear of belly buttons

Osmophobia: the fear of body odor

Peladophobia: the fear of bald people

Phalacrophobia: the fear of becoming bald

Phobophobia: the fear of phobias

WHAT'S EATING YOU?

MRSA stands for methicillin-resistant bacteria—*Staphylococcus aureus*. It is commonly called the "flesh-eating bacterium."

MRSA most frequently colonizes the nostrils, along with the respiratory and urinary tracts, and open wounds.

Each year, about eighteen thousand Americans die from MRSA.

Artificial turf burns suffered by football players are particularly susceptible to MRSA infections. One study found that high school football players suffer MRSA infections at sixteen times the national average.

SMALLPOX, BIG PROBLEM

The word "vaccine" was inspired by Edward Jenner's 1796 use of the pus from cowpox blisters to inoculate a young boy, giving him a mild case of cowpox, but immunizing him from the deadly smallpox. *Vacca* is Latin for "cow."

Throughout world history, it is estimated the one billion people have died from smallpox.

Smallpox was eradicated in 1980.

The Centers for Disease Control and Prevention and the Russian bioweapons program keep the only known living cultures of smallpox.

The Soviets mass-produced smallpox and had ICBM warheads capable of delivering it to the United States.

TICKED OFF

Lyme disease is named for the town of Lyme, Connecticut, where several early cases were diagnosed in 1975.

Only about 1 percent of tick "bites" result in the transmission of Lyme disease.

A tick must be attached to the skin for at least a day to transmit the disease.

HEART OF THE MATTER

The sound of a heartbeat is that of the heart valves slamming shut.

Heart muscle cells will continue to beat after being removed from the heart.

WHAT'S THAT?

Men are three times more likely to have noise-related hearing loss due to riding motorcycles, working with power tools, and using other loud equipment.

Thirteen percent of men age twenty to sixty-nine suffer from noise-induced hearing loss.

WISHFUL THINKING

Pseudocyesis is the medical term for "false pregnancy."

One notable sufferer from pseudocyesis was Queen Mary of England, who twice erroneously believed she was with child.

Women who experience false pregnancy are convinced that they are carrying a child. They even may exhibit physical symptoms, such as an enlarged abdomen, morning sickness, menstrual irregularity, tender breasts, and/or the sensation of a fetus moving inside them.

In 2010, a woman went to a North Carolina hospital believing she was going to give birth. The doctors did an ultrasound and found no heartbeat, so they induced labor. When no baby was forthcoming, they performed a C-section, only to find a normal uterus and no baby.

Cases of false pregnancy seemed to peak in the 1940s, when roughly 1 in 250 "pregnancies" were false.

Doctors still don't fully understand what causes pseudocyesis.

Dogs experience false pregnancies at a much higher rate than do humans.

Stranger still is Couvade syndrome, or sympathetic pregnancy in men. In these cases, a man close to a pregnant woman will experience many of her symptoms as the date of the delivery approaches. Men have been known to get big bellies, food cravings, and false labor pains, among other changes.

MYSTERY DIAGNOSIS

Gigantomastia is a rare condition where a woman's breasts grow to enormous size during puberty or after pregnancy. A rural Peruvian woman became bedridden when her size N breasts became too large for her to stand up without fainting. Surgeons removed thirty-five pounds of fat from her bosom, leaving her with 34B breasts.

Sleeping Beauty Syndrome, also known as Kleine-Levin Syndrome, is a condition wherein people become suddenly drowsy and may sleep for days or weeks at a time, only waking to eat or go to the bathroom.

A British woman suffered a severe migraine headache in 2010 and developed a case of Foreign Accent Syndrome. She now speaks with a Chinese accent.

Wernicke's aphasia is caused by damage to the brain's superior temporal gyrus. Sufferers sound as if they are speaking normally, but make no sense.

Face blindness, or prosopagnosia, is a neurological disorder where sufferers cannot recognize faces: not those of family and friends—in some cases, not even their own. Oddly, those with face blindness can recognize people by their clothes, body shapes, gaits, or voices.

Sirenomelia, or mermaid syndrome, is an extremely rare condition where the legs are fused together at birth. The colon and genitals are usually absent and life expectancy is very short.

One hundred Americans have been known to be afflicted with congenital insensitivity to pain (CIPA), where one has a gene mutation causing them to literally feel no pain. This may sound like a good thing, but suffers are more likely to die from trauma, as they might not realize the extent of injuries they may incur.

Aquagenic urticaria is a rare skin disorder where suffers are literally allergic to water. Ordinary water of any temperature will cause the skin to develop hives. Sufferers must bathe with distilled water.

Hyperthymestic syndrome is known to affect only one person in the world. The woman has total recall of every day in her adult life, including what she did, what the weather was like, and significant news stories of the day.

People with cataplexy pass out any time they experience strong emotions, such as fear, anxiety, embarrassment, awe, or exhilaration. Even laughing causes suffers to collapse.

Fish odor syndrome, also known as trimethylaminuria, makes the breath, sweat, and urine smell like fish.

Some people are allergic to the electromagnetic waves given off by cell phones, microwave ovens, and even some cars. Using or being near these devices causes a severe skin rash.

Sexsomnia compels suffers to engage in sex while asleep. Since they are not aware of it, the condition has been used to acquit defendants accused of rape or sexual assault in Canada and Great Britain.

Exploding-head syndrome sufferers experience loud, explosion-like sounds that seem to come from inside their brains shortly after falling asleep. The condition can come on suddenly and may go away just as quickly.

Fatal familial insomnia usually begins after age fifty. Plaques in the brain inhibit the ability to sleep, causing suffers to become psychotic and, eventually, to die in six months to three years.

Those with Moebius syndrome cannot move their facial muscles, so smiling, frowning, sucking, or even blinking the eyes is not possible.

Cystinosis is an extremely rare childhood condition where the amino acid cystine accumulates in the body's cells and turns to crystal. Affected organs include the eyes, kidneys, liver, muscles, pancreas, and brain. If left untreated, those afflicted will die of kidney failure.

NAME THAT DISEASE

Klinefelter syndrome, where males have an extra X chromosome, was named after Massachusetts endocrinologist Harry Klinefelter, who described it in 1942.

Parkinson's disease is named for English surgeon James Parkinson, who first worked with the disease in 1817.

Hodgkin's lymphoma, formerly known as Hodgkin's disease, is named for British physician Thomas Hodgkin, who first studied the disease in 1842.

Huntington's disease, or Huntington's chorea, was first studied in depth by twenty-two-year-old American physician George Huntington in 1872. The word "chorea" means "involuntary writhing movements." People of Western European descent are much more likely to carry the gene for this disease than are those of African or Asian descent.

Children of a parent with Huntington's disease have a 50 percent chance of contracting it themselves.

MANEUVER MAN

The Heimlich maneuver was first written about in the medical journal *Emergency Medicine*, by American physician Henry Jay Heimlich in 1974. After the article appeared, the first choking person's life was saved using the maneuver in a Bellevue, Washington, restaurant.

Although the maneuver is named for Heimlich, there is some disagreement as to whether he invented it.

The Heimlich maneuver is not the preferred first response to a choking person anymore. The American Red Cross now recommends striking a conscious choking victim on the back five times to dislodge an obstruction. If this does not work, then five abdominal thrusts should be employed. (They don't even call it the Heimlich maneuver anymore.)

WHAT AILS YOU

The AIDS virus is the leading killer of women between the ages of fifteen and forty-four worldwide. Unsafe sex is the primary cause.

Scarlet fever is so named for the bright red color the tongue turns on those afflicted with this bacterial infection. The tongue resembles a strawberry, and the skin develops a red rash.

Yellow fever is a viral disease that gets its name from the liver damage it causes and the associated jaundice that turns the skin and the whites of the eyes yellow.

Whooping cough, or pertussis, is a bacterial disease named for the "whoop" sound that is made when air is inhaled into the lungs after a cough.

Fevers are useful because the heat increase may kill susceptible bacteria and viruses and may also increase the activity of white blood cells.

During the Renaissance, obesity was considered a status symbol.

MEDICAL MISCELLANY

According to the Centers for Disease Control and Prevention, the average annual medical bill for obese patients is $4,871, whereas healthy-weight patients' bills average $3,442 per year.

Like blood banks, there are now breast milk banks that collect and store breast milk for mothers who cannot produce their own. All donated milk is tested, pasteurized, and frozen until needed.

A 2010 American Medical Association study found that 70 percent of depressed people get no benefit from taking antidepressants.

SPORTS AUTHORITY

THE THRILL OF VICTORY . . .

The UCLA men's basketball team held the all time NCAA record for consecutive wins at eighty-eight, set between 1971 and 1974. In December 2010, the University of Connecticut's women's basketball team broke UCLA's record, by winning its eighty-ninth game in a row. They extended that streak to ninety games before losing to Stanford.

The UCLA men's volleyball team holds the record for most NCAA championships—nineteen.

THE AGONY OF DEFEAT

During the 1972–73 NBA season, the Philadelphia 76ers set the single-season mark for worst record—9–73.

The Tampa Bay Buccaneers joined the NFL in 1976. They lost every game that first season and the first twelve games of their second season, going 0–26, before winning their first game.

The 1899 Cleveland Spiders set the Major League Baseball record for futility, going 20–134. They finished 84 games out of first place.

In more recent times, the 1962 New York Mets went 40–120, finishing 60½ games out of first place.

In hockey, the 1974–75 NHL Washington Capitols had a final record of 8-67-5.

Cleveland professional sports teams have not won a championship in the last forty-seven years.

AMERICA'S PASTIME?

Eighty percent of the players in the National Hockey League come from countries other than America. Twenty-eight percent of Major League Baseball players are non-Americans. Only 3 percent of National Football League players are from other countries.

THREE YARDS AND A CLOUD OF DUST

Running backs have the shortest careers of players at any NFL position. They average about eight years in the league.

A running back can be a halfback, a fullback, or a tailback. Traditionally, a halfback lines up halfway between the line of scrimmage and the fullback. (A quarterback lines up a quarter of the way from the line of scrimmage and the fullback.) Today, since a halfback is usually a team's primary runner, and the fullback is used for blocking, the halfback lines up behind the fullback and becomes a tailback.

COACHES' CORNER

In his thirteen years as head coach of the Notre Dame football team from 1918 to 1930, Knute Rockne compiled the highest winning percentage of any coach in the history of Division I-A—88.2 percent—with a record of 105-12-5.

Rockne died in a plane crash in Kansas in 1931 after just completing two undefeated seasons.

Paul Brown founded both the Cleveland Browns and the Cincinnati Bengals.

The Browns entered the NFL in 1950 and defeated the two-time defending champion Philadelphia Eagles, 35–10 in their first game. Philadelphia coach Greasy Neale disparaged the Browns, saying that all they could do was pass the ball. In the rematch between the two teams, later that same season, the Browns set a record that still stands, beating the Eagles 13–7 and not passing the ball one time.

Paul Brown introduced facemasks to pro football. He also was the first coach to use radio transmitters to communicate with players on the field.

Brown's offenses were the predecessor of the West Coast offense so popular today.

The Cincinnati Bengals play in Paul Brown Stadium.

John Madden was drafted by the Philadelphia Eagles in the twenty-first round in 1958, but a knee injury prevented him from ever playing pro ball. He played offensive tackle in college.

While Madden coached the Oakland Raiders (1969–78) they reached the AFC championship game seven times, losing five of them.

Madden developed his well-known fear of flying after suffering a panic attack on a 1979 flight. Since then he has traveled the country in a big customized bus/motor home.

Ironically, his wife, Virginia, is a licensed pilot.

BUCKING BRONKO

Chicago Bears player Bronko Nagurski's real first name was Bronislau.

He is the only professional football player to be named All-Pro at three different non-kicking positions—running back, offensive tackle, and defensive lineman.

At size 19½, his NFL championship ring is the largest ever.

Aside from a stellar football career with the Chicago Bears, Nagurski had a second career as a professional wrestler, where he won the world championship three times.

AUTOMATIC OTTO

Quarterback Otto Graham led the NFL Cleveland Browns to five straight title games during his tenure with the team from 1946 to 1955.

Graham's .810 winning percentage is the highest of any NFL quarterback.

Graham also won a National Basketball League title with the Rochester Royals in 1946.

MR. TOUCHDOWN

Sid Luckman quarterbacked the Chicago Bears to NFL titles in 1940, 1941, 1943, and 1946.

His career touchdown-to-pass-attempt ratio of 7.9 percent is the best ever. In 1943, he threw a touchdown on 13.9 percent of his pass attempts. He threw for seven touchdowns in one game in that same year.

Luckman led the league in yards per pass attempt a record seven times.

TRIPLE THREAT

Sammy Baugh quarterbacked the Washington Redskins from 1937 to 1952. He also played defensive back and punted. In 1943, he became the only player to lead the league in passing, punting (45.9 yard average), and interceptions (11).

His 51.4 yard punting average in 1940 remains the best ever season average.

THE GOLDEN ARM

Johnny Unitas was drafted by the Pittsburgh Steelers in 1955, but he was released from training camp because they had too many quarterbacks.

Unitas was a walk-on with the Baltimore Colts in 1956.

Unitas's first NFL pass was intercepted and returned for a touchdown. On his next play, he fumbled the ball away on a bad handoff.

He went on to establish a record that most experts believe will never be broken—forty-seven consecutive games with a touchdown pass.

BROWNS' BROWN

Jim Brown, who played running back for the Cleveland Browns from 1957 to 1965, was voted the Greatest Football Player Ever by the *Sporting News* in 2002.

He averaged 104.3 yards per game and 5.2 yards per carry for his career, still the NFL record.

Not only is Brown in the Football Hall of Fame, but he is also in the Lacrosse Hall of Fame.

THE GRAND OLD MAN

Quarterback and placekicker George Blanda holds the NFL record for most seasons played—twenty-six.

He made 943 of 959 extra points attempted.

At 48 years and 109 days, Blanda was the oldest player ever in an NFL game.

George Blanda was the first ever pick in a fantasy football league.

SMITHS AND JONES

In the 2008–09 season there were fifty Williams, forty-seven Johnsons, forty-four Smiths, thirty-five Browns, twenty-seven Jones, and twenty Jacksons listed on NFL rosters.

FIT TO BE TIED

The NFL first started playing overtime games in 1974. Before this, games tied at the end of regulation ended in a tie.

Seventy percent of overtime games are decided by field goals. Four percent still end in ties.

WINTER WARRIORS

Iceland, despite its name, has never won a Winter Olympics medal.

Norway is the all time Winter Olympics medal winner.

Over one million Canadians participate in the sport of curling.

The price of one set of curling rocks is $7,000.

THE GREAT ONES

Former NHL hockey star Wayne Gretzky (the "Great One") leads all major American team sports players with nine Most Valuable Player awards. Barry Bonds had seven Major League Baseball MVPs, Kareem Abdul-Jabbar had six NBA MVPs, and Peyton Manning has four NFL MVPs (and counting).

The only numbers retired by a major professional American sports league are Wayne Gretzky's number 99 by the National Hockey League and Jackie Robinson's number 42 by Major League Baseball.

Steffi Graf spent the most weeks (377) ranked as the number one women's tennis player. Second on the list is Martina Navratilova (332), and third is Chris Evert (260). Martina Hingis (209) and Monica Seles (178) round out the top five.

BATTER UP

Ash is used to make baseball bats because it is stronger, lighter, and more flexible than other woods.

RUBBING MUD

Brand-new baseballs have a shiny finish that can cause wild pitches.

Before the 1930s, players would rub tobacco juice or shoe polish on the balls to dull them down.

In 1938, ex-ballplayer Lena Blackburne discovered a clay soil on the banks of a tributary to the Delaware River somewhere in New Jersey (the exact site is still kept secret). He marketed it to major league teams as the perfect dirt to rub on new balls to degloss them. Lena Blackburne's Baseball Rubbing Mud has been used by every major league team.

There is actually a member of every team's clubhouse staff whose job it is to rub the dirt on a few dozen balls before each game.

BRONX BOMBERS

The New York Yankees first added pinstripes to their uniforms in 1912.

The Yankees' "NY" insignia was designed in 1877 by Louis B. Tiffany for a medal to be given to the first New York City policeman to be shot in the line of duty.

The Yankees have retired fifteen numbers, the most of any Major League Baseball team.

Thirty-six former Yankees players have been inducted in the Hall of Fame.

TIGRRR

Tiger Woods was born Eldrick Tont Woods. His father, a retired Army colonel and Vietnam vet, started calling him "Tiger" in honor of a friend in the South Vietnamese army that he had given the same nickname.

Woods is half Asian (one-quarter Chinese and one-quarter Thai), one-quarter African American, one-eighth Dutch, and one-eighth Native American. He refers to himself as "Cablinasian," a word he coined for Caucasian, Black, Indian, and Asian.

TENNIS, ANYONE?

The proper name for the Grand Slam tennis tournament at Wimbledon, England, is The Championships Wimbledon.

It is held at the All-England Lawn Tennis and Croquet Club. The club, as the name implies, was originally a croquet club. Tennis was first played there in 1875, and the first championship was held in 1877.

The ball boys and girls are chosen from local schools. Girls have been used since 1977.

Ball boys and girls are paid between £120 and £160 for the thirteen day tournament.

The courts are exclusively rye grass.

Up until 1975, the U.S. Open was also played on grass, as was the Australian Open, until 1988.

DIRTY POOL

Nelson Piquet Jr., a driver for Renault's Formula 1 racing team, intentionally crashed his car during the 2008 Singapore Grand Prix to allow a teammate to make up lost time when the race was delayed to clean up the debris.

In the 1976 Montreal Olympics, Soviet pentathlete Boris Onischenko was disqualified for rigging his epee sword with a mechanism that would indicate that he had scored a hit whenever he wanted.

During the 1961 college basketball season, Columbia player Jack Molinas and thirty-six other players from twenty-two teams were arrested for working with the mob to fix games. Molinas, who was at the center of the scheme, later played one season with the NBA's Fort Wayne Pistons, but was suspending for gambling.

EXTRA POINTS

In a recent survey, 17 percent of American adults admitted to peeing in pools. Even fourteen-time Olympic gold medalist Michael Phelps has confessed to doing so.

In 2010, thirteen-year-old American Jordan Romero became the youngest person to summit Mount Everest.

Bobby Orr was the only National Hockey League defenseman to lead the league in scoring, and he did so twice.

It takes forty miles of tubing to deliver the beverages to the taps at Lincoln Financial Field in Philadelphia.

The ancient Greeks used to box sitting down, facing one another. The boxers would beat each other until one of them died. Later, Greek boxers would fight standing up, in the nude, wearing only spiked gloves.

Cheerleading is by far the most dangerous female sport, followed by gymnastics and track.

Sixty-eight percent of office workers bet on Super Bowl office pools. Another 56 percent bet on the March Madness NCAA basketball tournament, and 34 percent join office lottery ticket pools.

The Indianapolis Motor Speedway was built in 1906 by Carl Fisher as a research facility to test cars.

LIVING PLANET

DRY DATA

It takes a saguaro cactus two hundred years to reach its full height of forty-five feet.

Native Americans used the cactus to build homes.

Saguaros grow only in the Sonoran Desert of Arizona, California, and Mexico. There are none to be found in Texas, New Mexico, Nevada, Utah, or Colorado.

The nearest saguaro to El Paso, Texas, is 250 miles away (regardless of what the Old El Paso brand label would seem to indicate).

The Sonoran Desert is the only habitat in the United States that supports jaguars.

More people die in the desert from drowning in flash floods than from heat exhaustion or thirst.

UP A TREE

In some years, oak trees don't produce any acorns. In others, they can produce up to ten thousand.

The autumn leaf color change in North America is visible from outer space.

SALT LOVERS

Mangrove trees can live in water twice as salty as the ocean. They have pores on their roots that filter out between 90 and 97 percent of the salt in seawater.

Mangroves use older leaves to collect and exude any salt that doesn't get filtered out by the roots. These leaves turn yellow and fall off, taking the salt with them.

MONKEY BUSINESS

Ring-tailed lemur males have special sex-scent glands on their wrists that they rub on their tails to entice prospective mates.

Orangutans make umbrellas out of branches.

Orangutan moms nurse their babies for six or seven years. That's the longest for any animal.

Chimpanzees remain fertile as long as humans.

Chimpanzees are more dangerous to humans than gorillas are.

🐿 MONKEY SEE, MONKEY DO

Tufted Capuchin monkeys are the cute little guys that are most often associated with organ grinders.

These monkeys, in the wild, will peel palm nuts and let them dry for several days in the sun so that they become brittle. The monkeys will then take the nuts to a large flat rock and crack open the nuts with very hard stones that they collect from a river one mile away. This is not an innate practice, but is learned when younger monkeys observe older ones.

Tufted Capuchin monkeys also crush millipedes, which they rub on their backs as a natural mosquito repellant.

These monkeys are so smart that they have been trained to assist quadriplegics by opening doors, microwaving food, and opening bottles for them.

SEA WORLD

A starfish, or sea star, can regrow a lost arm in three weeks.

Starfish have two stomachs, one of which can be everted to engulf prey.

Corals appear passive, but in fact they wage fierce battles against adjacent corals by extending their stomach threads to digest their neighbors.

The Great Barrier Reef, at 1,200 miles long, is the largest living thing on the planet.

An East Coast sea slug has been discovered that swipes genes from algae and then produces its own chlorophyll. It can then live the rest of its life without eating, by simply basking in sunlight, just like a plant.

The largest squid ever hauled up from the depths of the sea was thirty-one feet long and weighed more than one thousand pounds.

Jellyfish have no brains or blood.

A sea louse female is lured by a male into a burrow for mating, where there may be twenty-five others in his harem. To add injury to insult, once her young are mature, they will eat her from the inside out.

A FAREWELL TO ARMS

An octopus is able to unscrew the lid of a jar to get to food within.

Octopi are more closely related to oysters and snails than to any other animals.

Octopus mothers will guard their fifty thousand eggs for forty days before they hatch. To sustain themselves during this period of time in which they can't hunt, these ladies may eat one of their arms.

STAY OUT OF THE WATER!

The geographic cone snail of the seas of the Indo-Pacific has venom that works almost instantaneously, because the slow-moving creature would have no chance of tracking down its prey otherwise.

One species of cone snail is nicknamed the cigarette snail, because a person is said to only have time enough to smoke a cigarette after being stung by one before he will die.

A protein in the cone snail's venom has been found to be ten thousand times more effective a painkiller than morphine, without the risk of addiction.

The box jellyfish, which also swims the waters of the Indo-Pacific, has a venom in its tentacles that kills fish instantly, so that its prey does not damage its delicate tentacles. The toxin it injects is so powerful that humans stung by this jelly are sometimes too paralyzed to make it to shore and die of drowning or heart failure.

The venom of the blue-ringed octopus comes from bacteria that live in its salivary glands.

Irukandji, thumbnail-sized jellyfish found in the waters off Queensland, Australia, are among the most venomous creatures in the world. One sting from these tiny beasts is enough to kill an adult.

FISH STORIES

Cichlids are fish that carry their eggs and hatchlings in their mouths. Cuckoo catfish will wait for a cichlid to lay its eggs and will quickly dart in and deposit its own eggs among the cichlid eggs. The cichlid then, unknowingly, takes all the eggs into its mouth. The catfish eggs will hatch first, and the catfish fry will eat the cichlid young as they hatch.

Fish can get tuberculosis and herpes.

Owners of expensive fish can have laser surgery done on them to remove cancers, followed up with chemotherapy.

FLIPPER FACTS

Dolphins have beaks (long snouts), while porpoises do not. Dolphins also have more prominent dorsal fins and much more pointy teeth than do porpoises.

Dolphins in Florida Bay will swim around a school of fish in shallow water and disturb the bottom with their tails, creating a ring of mud around the fish. The fish then jump out of the water to escape the ring and are caught in midair by the waiting sea mammals.

FROGGY FACTS

Amphibians have smooth skin and no claws. Reptiles have scaly skin and claws.

The pebble toad of Venezuela has a unique form of self-defense. When threatened, this amphibian will fold up its limbs tightly against its body and roll down a slope, or right off a rocky cliff, to get away.

The common wood frog freezes solid every winter and thaws out every spring to mate.

A new species of bird-eating frog with fangs was found in Thailand, in 2008.

THEY NEED A THICK SKIN

The word "pachyderm" is from the Greek words meaning "thick skin."

Elephants, hippos, and rhinos are all commonly known as pachyderms. The classification is considered archaic today.

HUMAN FISH

An olm is a sightless, unpigmented amphibian that lives in the total darkness of subterranean cave waters in the Italy-Croatia-Slovenia region.

Olms are known locally as the "human fish," because their skin color is very similar to that of Caucasians.

Olms never really develop out of the larval stage, spending their entire lives, which can reach up to one hundred years, underwater.

As an adaptation to scarcity of food supplies, olms can live for ten years without eating.

Olms are considered a symbol of Slovenian heritage and have been depicted on the country's coins.

MONSTER MASH

The Gila monster is the only venomous lizard native to the United States. It is also the largest lizard species native to America.

Gila monsters eat only five to ten times a year.

Gilas are a protected species in Arizona and Nevada.

DOGGONE IT

There are roughly 400 million dogs in the world.

The largest, longest, and heaviest dog ever recorded was Zorba, an English mastiff, who was eight feet, three inches long, stood thirty-seven inches at the shoulder, and weighed 343 pounds, the size of a large donkey.

Ancients believed that if one ingested a hair from a dog that had bitten them, they would be protected from infection. This is probably the origin of treating a hangover by drinking "the hair of the dog that bit you."

Dogs can be trained to recognize the smell of breast and lung cancers, and to recognize several types of ovarian cancers.

Breeds such as spaniels, retrievers, setters, pointers, terriers, collies, scent hounds, and corgis all originated in the British Isles.

Basenjis are known as the "barkless" dogs. Instead of barking, they produce yodeling sounds.

Basset hounds have the largest bones for their body size of any breed of dog.

The word "basset" derives from the French *bas*, meaning "low."

"Corgi" means "dwarf dog" in Welsh.

Ibizan hounds are believed to have descended from dogs bred in Egypt in 3400 BC.

A German tax collector named Ludwig Dobermann bred a vicious guard dog to accompany him on his rounds. The dog is the Doberman pinscher (note the single "n").

The bichon frise was bred in the Middle Ages as a lap dog to attract fleas from its owner.

The German shepherd and the Chow Chow are the top two biting dogs.

A golden retriever's mouth is so "soft" that it can pick up three raw eggs without breaking them.

The world's oldest dog—Chanel, a wire-haired dachshund from Long Island—died at the ripe old age of twenty-one in 2010.

HERE, SPOT

There is no proof that Dalmatians originated in Dalmatia.

Dalmatians were bred as carriage dogs—canines that would trot along beside horse drawn carriages and guard them when the owner was away. They were used by early firefighters for this purpose and remain the firefighter's dog, especially in the United States.

Thirty percent of Dalmatians suffer from partial or total hearing loss.

Boxers, bull terriers, Great Danes, and poodles also have a high propensity for deafness.

DASHER AND DANCER

Over the course of a reindeer's lifetime, it will travel some seventy-five thousand miles.

Reindeer hooves change with the season. In summer, when the tundra is wet and muddy, the hooves become soft for extra traction. In winter, when the ground freezes over, the hooves become hard to bite into the snow. Hard hooves also allow the animals to dig down in the snow to reach buried vegetation.

BIG BIRD

An ostrich egg is so strong that it can support the weight of a two-hundred-pound person.

An ostrich egg contains two thousand calories.

It takes forty minutes to hard boil an ostrich egg.

Ostrich racing is popular on the Arabian Peninsula, where children are used as jockeys.

HUMMERS

A hummingbird's heart beats six hundred times per minute when it is active and drops to thirty-six beats per minute at night. It also reduces its body temperature by half at night to conserve energy.

Insects are a hummer's main source of protein.

The male and female purple-throated Carib hummingbirds of Dominica have different-shaped beaks and feed on different kinds of flowers to reduce competition.

In order to fly backward, hummers beat their wings in a figure-eight pattern.

FEELING SLUGGISH

Snails can have hundreds to thousands of teeth.

Aside from the absence of a shell, there is not much difference between a slug and a snail.

Some snails live in the desert.

CAT TALES

Cats have been domesticated for about half as long as have dogs.

A cat loses almost as much body fluid through grooming as it does through urination.

The first domesticated cats came to America on the *Mayflower*.

The Maine coon cat is America's only native pure-bred cat.

Female cats are superfecund, which means each of the kittens in a litter may have a different father.

Cats that only eat dog food may go blind, as it doesn't contain the necessary nutrient taurine.

A cat purrs at the same frequency as an idling diesel engine.

Pure white, blue-eyed cats are often deaf.

The life expectancy of a cat in 1930 was eight years. It now is sixteen years.

Twenty percent of cats do not get "high" from catnip, as they lack the required gene.

Cats spend nearly 30 percent of their lives grooming. They spend about 65 percent of their time sleeping.

An English kitty holds the record for the largest litter—nineteen kittens—fifteen of which survived, in 1970.

A Texas tabby named Dusty gave birth to some 420 kittens. Not all at once, of course!

Creme Puff, another cat from the Lone Star State, lived to the ripe old age of thirty-eight.

Cats are successful in catching mice on about one third of their attempts.

Aspirin and antifreeze are deadly to cats. Garlic and onions are also bad for them.

Cats seem to like women better than men, probably because women have higher voices.

People aren't allergic to cat hair or dander but to sebum, a fatty substance secreted by the animal's sebaceous glands. Some people may be allergic to one cat, but not to another.

TIGGER, TOO

There are more captive tigers in the world than wild ones.

In the United States alone, there are about seven thousand "pet" big cats.

MAMMAL MOMMAS

Koala mothers feed their babies their own feces so that the little ones can acquire the bacteria their digestive tracts need to detoxify the highly poisonous eucalyptus leaves that they eat.

All the female elephants in a herd help moms tend their young.

Only 3 percent of mammals form long-term pair bonds.

SHIPS OF THE DESERT

A camel's body temperature is about 93°F at night, going up to 106°F during the day. It is only above this temperature that a camel will begin to sweat.

A camel's thick coat reflects the sunlight and insulates the body from the heat of the desert sand, helping to keep the animal cool.

A camel's gait suggests a rolling boat, which is why they are known as the "ships of the desert."

Camels can drink twenty-five gallons of water in one go.

Camels have two big toes with skin stretched between that keeps them from sinking into the sand.

Camels originated in North America 50 million years ago. About 3 million years ago, they migrated from Alaska into Siberia and down into Africa.

DUCKBILLS

A female platypus builds a nearly one-hundred-foot-long breeding burrow that she plugs with mud each time she leaves, to protect her young.

Female platypuses don't have teats. They exude milk from pores in the skin, which pools in its folds, and is licked up by the young.

Baby platypuses are born with teeth, but soon lose them, using horny plates to grind their food.

BUZZ OFF

The Dawson's burrowing bee of Australia's Outback is one of the only animals that regularly kills its own. The males of this species all arrive at the same time that the females are emerging from their burrows. The males go into a killing frenzy to breed with the females. When it is all over, every male bee is dead, and so are many females.

There are at least 120,000 species of fly.

Argentine grass-cutting ants carry blades of grass underground where they use them to grow a fungus that the ants eat. The ants put antibiotics on the grass, which inhibit all fungi, except the kind they eat, from growing. This particular fungus is found nowhere else but in the ant colonies.

Bombardier beetles produce hydrogen peroxide and hydroquinone in separate chambers on their abdomens. When threatened, these chemicals come together in a third chamber and react to form a boiling hot liquid (212°F) that the beetles squirt in self-defense. The intense heat can kill other insects or burn human skin.

The longest insect is a species of walking stick that measures thirteen inches.

It is well known that monarch butterflies migrate from the United States to overwinter in Mexico. It is less well known that the migration doesn't occur in one generation, but over the course of several.

Monarch larvae can only eat milkweed plants. However, up to two-thirds of the little caterpillars die in their first day of life from becoming entrapped in the sticky, milky sap of this plant.

The crab spider can dive beneath water using an air bubble it keeps on its back to breathe.

DINOSAUR DIGEST

The word "dinosaur" was coined in 1842 by English paleontologist Richard Owen. It derives from the Greek words *deinos*, meaning "powerful, terrible, or wondrous," and *sauros*, meaning "lizard."

About twenty new dinosaur species are discovered each year.

Some dinos had two brains—one in the head and one in the tail.

Dinosaurs are believed to have slept with their heads under their arms, much like some modern-day birds.

Dinosaurs swallowed small stones to aid in digestion.

WILD SEX

Female crickets will mark a male with their scent during sex to make sure they never have sex with that male again.

Fruit bats will copulate while hanging upside down, and the female may perform oral sex on the male.

Scorpion males place their sperm packets on a stalk sticking out of the ground and push the female until she is over it to inseminate her.

ILLEGAL IMMIGRANTS

Researchers estimate that there are fifty thousand invasive (non-native) species of life in the United States.

WAR, WHAT IS IT GOOD FOR?

IN THE CROSSHAIRS

The greatest sniper of all time was Finnish soldier Lance Corporal Simo Häyhä. During the 1939–40 Winter War between Finland and the Soviet Union, Häyhä killed an estimated 542 Soviet troops with a rifle, averaging five kills a day. He also took out two hundred more with a machine gun.

Soviet sniper Junior Lieutenant Vasily Zaytsev, made famous in the movie *Enemy at the Gates*, racked up 225 German kills during the Battle of Stalingrad.

Chinese sniper Zhang Taofang killed 214 in thirty-two days without a sniper scope during the Korean War.

American Gunnery Sergeant Carlos Hathcock had ninety-three confirmed and two hundred probable kills in the Vietnam War. His distance record of making a kill at 2,500 yards lasted until 2002.

U.S. Marine Chuck Mawhinney had 103 confirmed kills in Vietnam and another 203 probables. In one engagement, he eliminated sixteen Vietcong crossing a river in thirty seconds with a semiautomatic rifle.

U.S. Staff Sergeant Timothy Kellner had 139 confirmed kills and another one hundred probable kills in Operation Iraqi Freedom.

American Delta Force snipers Master Sergeant Gary Gordon and Sergeant First Class Randy Shughart were featured in the film *Black Hawk Down*. They requested to be inserted to protect the crew of a downed U.S. helicopter from numerous attacking Somalis. Armed with only their sniper rifles and sidearms, they fought their way to the copter and held off the Somalis until their ammunition ran out. Before being killed, the two took out twenty-four Somalis, with many more critically or mortally wounded.

SNIPER STOPPER

The Soldier Wearable Acoustic Targeting System (SWATS) is an iPod-sized device that can pinpoint the location of a sniper one-tenth of a second after a bullet has been fired. It is deployed with American troops in Iraq and Afghanistan.

INTO THE WILD BLUE YONDER

In 1924, the U.S. Air Service (forerunner to the U.S. Army Air Corps, the U.S. Army Air Force, and eventually the U.S. Air Force) had nine hundred pilots and 330 crashes.

IN THE BUFF

The B-52 Stratofortress long-range bomber came into service with the U.S. Air Force in 1955. It carried nuclear weapons and was supposed to act as a deterrent to a Soviet attack.

> The plane is known in military circles as the BUFF, or "Big, Ugly, Fat Fucker."

During the Cold War, there were nuclear-armed B-52s in the air twenty-four hours a day, 365 days a year.

> There have been numerous crashes of B-52s carrying nuclear bombs—including ones in Maryland, North Carolina, and California. Luckily, there were no detonations.

A 1966 crash in Spain and a 1968 crash in Greenland did release plutonium and uranium from the weapons that hit the ground, which the United States had to clean up at great expense.

> The B-52 can carry seventy thousand pounds of weapons.

During the Vietnam War, B-52s flew 130,000 bombing sorties.

In Operation Desert Storm, B-52s flew from an air-base in Louisiana to Iraq, delivered their payloads, and flew back to Louisiana without landing. The thirty-five hour, fourteen-thousand-mile round trip set a world record for longest combat mission.

The B-52 was only supposed to remain in active service for ten years. At present, the Air Force plans to keep some B-52s in service until 2040.

THAT'S THE SPIRIT

The B-2 Stealth Bomber is known as the Spirit.

The total program cost of each of these planes was $2.1 billion (in 1997 dollars).

Twenty-one B-2s were built, of which twenty survive today.

A B-2 can attack eighty different targets at one time, using its eighty five-hundred-pound JDAM-GPS-guided bombs.

BLACKBIRD FLY

The SR-71 "Blackbird," used by the U.S. Air Force from 1964 to 1998, still holds the record for fastest manned air-breathing aircraft, at 2,194 miles per hour.

The "SR" stands for "strategic reconnaissance."

Twelve of the thirty-two aircraft produced crashed in accidents.

The faster the Blackbird flew, the less fuel it burned per mile traveled, because of its engines' ramjet effect.

EYES IN THE SKIES

One third of the U.S. military's remote-controlled Predator drones flying missions over Afghanistan, Iraq, Pakistan, and Yemen have crashed. Pilots up to eight thousand miles away in the United States sit at computer screens and fly these planes.

If a Predator loses contact with its pilot, it will automatically return to base and land itself.

BOMBS AWAY

During World War II, nine thousand bombs had to be dropped on a target to have a 90 percent chance of hitting it.

A greater number of bombs were dropped on Laos during the Vietnam War than were dropped on Europe during World War II. More than one-half million bombing missions were flown over Laos.

Daisy cutters (BLU-82) were fifteen-thousand-pound bombs dropped in Vietnam to clear the jungle so helicopters would have a place to land.

Thermobaric bombs inject a fine, flammable mist into the surrounding air that creates a huge fireball and pressure wave that sucks the oxygen out of caves and tunnels, asphyxiating anyone hiding within. They have been used to great effect in Afghanistan.

BIG BANG

The first atomic bomb test blast, conducted in New Mexico in 1945, could be heard one hundred miles away. The light from the fireball could be seen 150 miles away, and windows were shattered 280 miles from the detonation.

One half of the energy of an atomic bomb is released in the air blast, 35 percent as heat and 15 percent as nuclear radiation.

Nuclear explosions create winds of 650 miles per hour.

A nuclear explosion can cause serious burns to people five miles away.

Hiroshima was selected as the target for the world's first atomic bomb during World War II because it was militarily important and because the United States intentionally hadn't conducted any previous bombings of the city, so that it was a "pristine" target and the effects of the bomb could be accurately assessed.

The Japanese surrendered to the Allies six days after a second nuclear bomb was dropped on Nagasaki on August 15, 1945. Had they not surrendered, the United States was prepared to drop another nuke on August 18 and to keep on dropping them as fast as they could be made.

An atomic bomb explosion is ten thousand times hotter than the surface of the sun.

MUTUALLY ASSURED DESTRUCTION

As of October 2010, Russia had 12,000 nuclear warheads and the United States had 9,400. France was estimated to have 300, China 240, Britain 185, Israel 80, Pakistan 70 to 90, and North Korea less than 10.

ANCHORS AWEIGH

The modern Nimitz class supercarriers, the biggest warships in the world, weigh one hundred thousand tons.

Because they are propelled by nuclear-powered engines, these carriers can travel the world's oceans for twenty years without refueling.

A Nimitz-class carrier has four bronze propellers, each weighing sixty-six thousand pounds, with a diameter of twenty-five feet.

The deck of an active aircraft carrier is considered by Lloyd's of London to be one of the most dangerous work environments.

In 1981, an EA-6B Prowler crashed onto the flight deck of the USS *Nimitz*, killing fourteen and injuring forty-five.

The first female Navy F-14 Tomcat pilot, Lieutenant Kara Hultgreen, was killed during a training landing on the deck of the *Abraham Lincoln* in 1994.

TANKS A LOT

It takes eight months to build an M1A2 Abrams tank, at a cost of $6 million.

The Abrams tank is named after General Creighton Abrams, former Army chief of staff and the commander of U.S. military forces in Vietnam from 1968 to 1972.

RUN SILENT, RUN DEEP

A nuclear-powered submarine never needs to refuel during its twenty-five year lifespan.

Only a few officers on board a U.S. submarine actually know where they are at any one time. Not even the helmsman (the person who steers the sub) or the commanders back on land know its exact location.

Sixty percent of sailors on American nuclear subs are between the ages of eighteen and twenty-two.

As of 2010, no women serve on U.S. submarines.

The U.S. Navy's Marine Mammals unit has trained sea lions to locate underwater bombs.

DAVY JONES'S LOCKER

There have been many accidents involving nuclear subs since they first entered service. The most notable follow:

In 1961, the Soviet nuclear submarine K-19's nuclear reactor almost melted down. Seven crewmen gave their lives to enter the reactor room and jury-rig a makeshift cooling system. Others on board also died from radiation exposure.

In 1969, the Soviet K-19 found itself in trouble again, hitting an American sub while two hundred feet down, sustaining severe damage.

A third tragedy occurred on the K-19 in 1972, when a fire broke out that killed twenty-eight sailors. Twelve men were trapped in the torpedo room for twenty-four days until the sub could be towed back to a base.

In 1968, another Soviet sub, the K-27, had a near meltdown that killed nine sailors.

In 1986, a third Soviet sub, K-219, almost had a meltdown at sea. It was only prevented when a nineteen-year-old sailor, Sergei Preminin, gave his life to manually lower the control rods. The sub was later scuttled with its complement of nuclear missiles still on board.

In 2000, the Russian sub *Kursk* (K-141) sank after the explosion of some of her torpedoes. Twenty-three members of the crew survived the blasts and were alive in the sub on the ocean floor for an undetermined length of time. The sub was later raised from the bottom and the bodies recovered.

In 1963, the American nuclear submarine USS *Thresher* was lost at sea. It is believed that a pipe burst that prevented the sub from surfacing, and she imploded upon sinking too deep.

In 1967, the USS *Scorpion* was lost at sea with all ninety-nine crew on board. It took six months to find the wreckage on the seabed, and no cause for the disaster has ever been found.

TEX-MEX

The states of Texas, California, Nevada, Arizona, Utah, and parts of New Mexico, Colorado, and Wyoming were added to the United States as a result of the Mexican-American War (1846–48).

American forces advanced all the way to Mexico City before Mexican leader Santa Anna surrendered.

Democrats in Congress tried to annex all of Mexico at the war's conclusion.

MAJOR PRODUCTION

At the end of World War II, the United States was producing three jeeps every four minutes.

America made three hundred thousand planes over the course of WWII.

WASPY LADIES

During World War II, more than one thousand American women were trained as Women Airforce Service Pilots (WASP).

WASP flew military aircraft from the factories where they were made to ports of embarkation. They also towed targets for live antiaircraft fire training. This freed up more male pilots to go fight in the war.

Thirty-eight WASP were killed during their time in the service. WASP killed in the line of duty had to be flown home at the family's expense and were denied the right to have a flag placed on their coffins.

In 2010, Barack Obama awarded the WASP the Congressional Gold Medal.

OLD BLOOD AND GUTS

George Patton was the first officer assigned to the brand-new U.S. Tank Corps, when it was formed during World War I.

Patton is famed for rushing his Third Army to engage the Germans and help win the Battle of the Bulge, saving the besieged American troops at Bastogne.

Patton awarded his chaplain a bronze star after the Battle of the Bulge for coming up with a prayer that he believed caused the weather to improve just before the attack.

TORA! TORA! TORA!

Japanese Naval Marshall General Isoroku Yamamoto, who planned the attack on Pearl Harbor, studied at Harvard University and the U.S. Naval War College.

The Japanese code words to indicate success of their attack on Pearl Harbor was *tora*, or "tiger."

Yamamoto was killed on the morning of April 18, 1943, after Allied code breakers had intercepted secret transmissions of his travel itinerary. American fighters intercepted his flight and shot down his plane over the Solomon Islands.

WAVE THE FLAG

The iconic photograph of the American flag being raised on Mount Suribachi during the battle of Iwo Jima was really the second flag raised there. The first flag was taken down as a souvenir for the Marine battalion that raised it. Photographer Joe Rosenthal arrived at the site just as the second, larger flag went up.

Of the six men in the photo (one is barely visible), five were Marines and one was a Navy corpsman. Three of them would die later in the battle for the island.

Both flags are now in the National Museum of the Marines.

During the battle for Okinawa, about one-quarter of the civilian population died, many from mass suicides encouraged by the Japanese forces there.

X-DAY

The planned Allied invasion of Japan in World War II was called X-Day.

The invasion of Kyushu on mainland Japan, scheduled to begin on November 1, 1945, was code-named Operation Olympic. Forty-two aircraft carriers were to have taken part in the largest naval armada ever assembled.

The invasion of Honshu, which was scheduled for March 1, 1946, and code-named Coronet, would have been the biggest amphibious assault in history, employing twice as many divisions as participated in the D-Day landings.

When Japan announced its surrender at the end of World War II, many Allied prisoners of war were executed and some Japanese soldiers committed suicide.

The last two known Japanese soldiers finally surrendered on Lubang Island in the Philippines and on the Indonesian island of Morotai, in 1974.

FORTS OF ALL SORTS

U.S. Army base Fort Hood in Texas is named for Confederate General John Bell Hood.

Other U.S. Army forts named after Confederate generals include Fort Lee (General Robert E. Lee) in Virginia, Fort A.P. Hill (Lieutenant General Ambrose Powell Hill) in Virginia, Fort Pickett (General George E. Pickett, leader of the disastrous Pickett's Charge at Gettysburg) in Virginia, Camp Forrest (General Nathan Bedford Forrest) in Tennessee, and Camp Wheeler (General Joseph Wheeler) in Georgia.

TURNING POINTS

The siege of Vicksburg ended in a Union victory on July 4, 1863, one day after the Union victory at the battle of Gettysburg. These two Confederate losses marked the turning point of the American Civil War.

The siege of Vicksburg lasted forty-eight days, after which thirty-one thousand Confederate soldiers surrendered.

The city of Vicksburg did not celebrate Independence Day for nearly eighty years after the siege.

The Battle of Gettysburg was the largest invasion of the United States ever. Seventy-five thousand Confederate soldiers entered Pennsylvania.

The residents of Gettysburg had dead and wounded totaling more ten times the population of the town to care for after the battle.

Only five thousand of the twelve thousand Confederates in Pickett's Charge survived the assault.

BROTHER AGAINST BROTHER

The death rate in Civil War army hospitals was 30 to 40 percent.

Sixty percent of the South lived in rural poverty following the Civil War.

Most Rebel troops were poor and did not own slaves.

Missouri was recognized by the Union *and* the Confederacy during the Civil War.

In 1863, Abraham Lincoln enacted a national draft to support the Civil War. However, those who paid a three hundred dollar "commutation fee" were exempt, as were those who hired a substitute to serve for them. This enraged citizens of New York City, fifty thousand of whom rioted for three days, burning and looting the East Side, and killing scores of blacks, whom they blamed for the war.

At the end of the Civil War there were 450 brothels in Washington, DC, to service the soldiers.

WINTER OF THEIR DISCONTENT

The Continental Army, under General George Washington, spent the winter of 1779–80 at Jockey Hollow, near Morristown, New Jersey. This was the coldest New Jersey winter in recorded history.

> Due to the frigid weather, and the lack of food and pay, the entire contingent from Pennsylvania mutinied. When the New Jersey line also later mutinied, Washington had them arrested and the leaders shot by their own men. There were no more mutinies after that.

While the winter spent at Valley Forge, Pennsylvania, was milder, the wet conditions at this encampment led to the deaths of two thousand men from disease.

THE WAR WITH MANY NAMES

North Korea and South Korea are technically still at war. A truce was declared in 1953, but there was never a peace treaty. This war is considered a "police action" in the United States, since Congress never formally declared it a war.

> In South Korea, it is known as the "6-2-5 War" because it began on June 25, 1950.

In North Korea it is know as the "Fatherland Liberation War."

> In China it is known as the "War to Resist American Aggression and Aid Korea."

Before the Chinese entered the war on the side of North Korea in 1950, President Harry Truman threatened to use atomic bombs, which he had sent to Korea, to repel a Chinese invasion.

There are still about 28,500 American troops stationed in South Korea.

The Korean Demilitarized Zone (DMZ), set up when the truce was declared, is the most heavily defended border in the world.

In 1968, thirty-one North Korean commandos crossed the DMZ into South Korea to kill President Park Chung Hee. Thirty of them died in the attempt, and many South Koreans and three Americans were killed. Since then, there have been dozens of North Korean incursions and many casualties.

TURNCOATS

Benedict Arnold began the Revolutionary War as a highly successful American general. After being passed over for promotions and being investigated by Congress about money they erroneously believed he owed them, he switched sides when America formed an alliance with the French, and began sending the British intelligence on American troop strength and movements while negotiating his defection.

In 1780, while still an American general, Arnold requested to command the Fort at West Point, which he then planned to hand over to the British. His scheme would have worked, but the plot was uncovered when a British officer was captured with papers incriminating Arnold. Arnold narrowly escaped and took command of British forces for the remainder of the war. He received six thousand pounds and a generous pension for defecting. After the war, he lived out his life in London.

The execution of Julius and Ethel Rosenberg in 1953 for selling nuclear secrets to the Soviets was the first time in U.S. history that civilians were given the death penalty for treason.

During World War II, an American traitor named William Joyce became a naturalized German citizen and began doing Nazi propaganda radio broadcasts aimed at demoralizing the British and Americans. He came to be known as Lord Haw-Haw. Joyce was arrested at the war's end and hanged for treason.

Maine native Mildred Gillars was better known as Axis Sally during World War II. She made propaganda broadcasts for the Germans, mostly having to do with convincing GIs that their wives and sweethearts were being unfaithful to them back home. American troops referred to her as "the Bitch of Berlin." She was convicted of treason but escaped the death penalty, serving twelve years in prison instead.

American Iva Toguri D'Aquino is better known as Tokyo Rose. She broadcast on a Japanese propaganda radio program, playing popular American tunes and talking to the troops. She never directly broadcast propaganda, but she got the GIs to listen to her program, which did feature propaganda by others. She was arrested after the war, but was released in Japan after having been found to have done nothing illegal. However, when she tried to return to the United States in 1949, influential American radio host Walter Winchell raised a fuss, and she was re-arrested, tried for treason, and served six years behind bars.

DOGS OF WAR

During World War I, forty thousand Americans donated their pet dogs to serve in the Armed Forces. Seventy-five thousand dogs were used as messengers and to locate bodies. Dogs were even trained to jump out of airplanes and parachute to the ground.

BETTER LATE THAN NEVER

In 2010, Germany finally paid off the last of its debts from World War I, for reparations they agreed to in the 1919 Treaty of Versailles for the damage done to Allied countries.

CAMO COUTURE

The French military was the first to use camouflage, designed by artists, in World War I.

GLOBAL PRESENCE

The United States has troops stationed in more than two-thirds of the world's nations.

HOME ON THE RANGE

WHERE THE BUFFALO ROAM

The American buffalo is more correctly known as the American bison (*Bison bison*).

At the time of the American Revolution, bison could be found as far east as central Pennsylvania.

During the height of the great buffalo hunts, eight thousand were being killed every day.

HIGH NOON

The gunfight at the O.K. Corral didn't take place at the O.K. Corral, but in a vacant lot behind the corral.

WANTED: DEAD OR ALIVE

Jesse James and his brother, Frank James, were Confederate guerillas before their gang began its infamous crime spree from 1866 to 1882.

The authorities never managed to capture Jesse. He was killed for reward money by one of his own gang, Bob Ford, who shot James in the back of the head while he was adjusting a picture in his home.

Bob Ford and his brother Charley starred in a touring stage show, recreating the killing of Jesse.

HOLE IN THE WALL

A Pennsylvania native, the Sundance Kid's given name was Harry Longabaugh. He picked up his nickname after serving time in Sundance, Wyoming, for horse theft.

Butch Cassidy was born Robert Leroy Parker.

Butch was the leader of the Hole-in-the-Wall Gang. The Hole-in-the-Wall Pass is in Johnson County, Wyoming. Its geographical features made it the perfect hideout for several gangs of outlaws between the 1860s and 1910s. The pass was virtually impossible for lawmen to sneak into undetected, and numerous posses were driven off after shootouts at the entrance.

Butch and Sundance committed the longest string of train robberies in American history.

Historians are not sure what became of Butch and Sundance. Some speculate that they died in a shootout with Bolivian troops after robbing a mine payroll in 1908.

TRIPLE BILL

Billy the Kid's real name was Henry McCarty.

Billy was reputed to have killed more than twenty men, but four seems to be the actual number.

William Frederick "Buffalo Bill" Cody killed 4,860 bison in just eight months, while under contract to furnish workers on the Kansas Pacific Railroad with meat.

At age fourteen, Cody was a rider for the Pony Express.

At the turn of the twentieth century, Buffalo Bill's Wild West shows, which featured Annie Oakley, Sitting Bull, and Wild Bill Hickok, were so famous internationally that Cody was one of the most recognizable people in the world.

James Butler "Wild Bill" Hickok is the first documented person to have killed another man in a quick-draw duel, in 1865. (They weren't nearly as common as depicted in the movies.)

As a lawman, Hickok killed several other men, including the accidental shooting of a deputy, which cost him his badge.

Wild Bill, a notorious gambler, was shot in the back of the head while playing cards in a saloon in Deadwood, Dakota Territory (present-day South Dakota), by a man supposedly avenging Hickok's killing of his brother.

Hickok's poker hand at the time of his death—eights and aces—is known as "dead man's hand."

In 1979, Wild Bill was inducted into the Poker Hall of Fame.

ANNIE GET YOUR GUN

Annie Oakley, born Phoebe Ann Mosey, was America's first true female superstar.

Annie's family was destitute, and she spent a few years living on a poor farm and would hunt game to help support her siblings.

When she was twenty-one, Oakley beat a professional in a shooting contest, a man she later married, and joined Buffalo Bill's Wild West Show, where she became a huge star.

In 1903, newspaperman William Randolph Hearst published a false story accusing Annie of stealing to support a cocaine habit. She eventually won fifty-four cases of libel against the offending papers.

COURTING CALAMITY

Martha Jane Cannary Burke, aka Calamity Jane, was a famed "Indian fighter."

She acquired her nickname for her warning to men that to cross her was to "court calamity."

Jane claimed to have married Wild Bill Hickok and borne his child, although many doubted this.

PREACHER'S SON

Outlaw and gunfighter John Wesley Hardin claimed to have killed forty-two men. While this number may be an exaggeration, he did kill several men in gunfights by the age of seventeen.

Friends of one of his victims lynched Hardin's brother and two cousins as payback.

His father was a Methodist minister in Texas. Hardin is named after the founder of the Methodist faith—John Wesley.

Hardin was only convicted of one killing and served seventeen years behind bars. While in prison, he found God and became the leader of the church Sunday school.

Like Wild Bill Hickok, Hardin was shot in the back of the head and killed while gambling in a saloon.

MEDICINE MAN

Sitting Bull was a Hunkpapa Lakota Sioux medicine man and war chief.

As a child he was called Slow. It was for his heroic actions in a war party against the Crow, at age fourteen, that he was given the name Sitting Bull.

Sitting Bull is most famous for the defeat of Union troops at Custer's Last Stand.

After this battle, Sitting Bull and his tribe lived in exile in Saskatchewan for several years. When he returned to the United States, he was placed at a government camp and was later killed by Federal forces attempting to arrest him.

ONE WHO YAWNS

Geronimo's Apache name was Goyahkla, which means "one who yawns." He was given the name Geronimo by the Mexican army after he repeatedly attacked them with a knife, ignoring the bullets flying all around him. The Mexicans cried out to Saint Jerome for help—"Jeronimo!" The reason for his savage attack was to avenge the killing of his mother, wife, and children by said Mexicans.

Geronimo was thought to have had special powers because he survived many wounds from gunshots.

Legend has it that Prescott Bush, the father of President George H. W. Bush, and some of his fellow Yale Skull and Bones society friends, dug up the skull of Geronimo while stationed at Fort Sill, Oklahoma, during World War I and sent it back to the club in New Haven, Connecticut, where it remains today.

GUN THAT WON THE WEST

The Winchester 1873 was known as "The Gun That Won the West," because so many of them were sold to settlers in the American West.

WILL THAT BE CASH OR E-ZPASS?

When the homesteaders were settling the American West, Native Americans would charge them tolls to cross rivers and travel on roads.

POLITICS AS USUAL

VEEPS

The annual salary of the vice president of the United States is $227,300.

> The vice president's only official purpose, aside from filling in for a dead or disabled president, is to act as the president of the Senate. In this role, the VP casts a vote in the event of a tie.

Richard Nixon is the only non-sitting vice president to have been elected president.

> John Calhoun was the first vice president to resign his office. He did so to become a senator.

FDR was the first president to pick his running mate. Before this, party conventions chose the vice presidential candidate.

CREEPS

The group that was behind the Watergate break-in was known as the Committee to Re-elect the President, more appropriately known as CREEP.

G. Gordon Liddy was the "mastermind" of the Watergate Hotel break-in that led to the downfall of President Richard Nixon.

Liddy was sentenced to prison for twenty years, but only served four and a half, after President Jimmy Carter commuted his sentence. He now hawks gold on TV commercials and has a syndicated radio talk show.

GEORGES AND JAMESES

There have been six U.S. presidents named James, four named William, four named John, and three named George.

GEORGE THE FIRST

George and Martha Washington had no children together. George did, however, become stepfather to Martha's son and daughter from her first marriage.

George's stepson, John Parke Custis, died while serving in the Continental Army, shortly after Cornwallis surrendered at Yorktown, from a fever, preventing Washington from enjoying the victory that essentially ended the Revolutionary War.

George Washington was the only American president who didn't serve in Washington. He did, however, briefly live in White House, the plantation owned by Martha near Williamsburg, Virginia.

> George Washington checked out two library books that are now 220 years overdue. He checked out *Law of Nations* and a book on debates in the British House of Commons, which were due back at New York Society Library on November 2, 1789.

Washington only had one tooth left by the time he became president. He likely lost them from taking mercury oxide to treat malaria and smallpox.

THE ONLY THING WE
HAVE TO FEAR . . .

Franklin Delano Roosevelt borrowed his famous line, "The only thing we have to fear, is fear itself," from Francis Bacon, who wrote four hundred years earlier, "Nothing is to be feared, but fear itself."

> The Roosevelt family name is an Anglicized spelling of the Dutch Van Rosevelt (or Van Rosenvelt), meaning "from field of roses."

The van Rosevelts came to New Amsterdam (present-day New York) in the 1640s.

FDR was distantly related to James Monroe, Benedict Arnold, and John Smith Jr. (founder of the Mormon religion).

FDR's maternal grandfather made the family fortune in the opium trade.

FDR had six children with his wife, Eleanor, who considered sex "an ordeal to be endured."

FDR had an affair with Eleanor's social secretary, Lucy Mercer, which lasted from 1914 until he died in 1945. Eleanor found out about it in 1918 and offered to divorce Franklin so that he could be with Mercer, but his mother threatened to cut him off and Mercer, a Catholic, drew the line at marrying a divorced man with five kids.

After discovering his infidelity, Eleanor began living in a separate house.

ASK NOT WHAT YOUR COUNTRY CAN DO FOR YOU . . .

Cicero uttered the famous words "Ask not what your country can do for you, but rather what you can do for your country" two thousand years before John F. Kennedy did so.

JFK's elder brother, Joseph P. Kennedy Jr., was the son that their father, Joseph P. Kennedy Sr., was originally grooming to become president. However, Junior was killed on a bombing mission during World War II and the mantle fell to John.

The mission that killed Junior was named Aphrodite. Stripped-down bombers were loaded with explosives and flown to targets with another plane following close behind. When the bomber was near the target, the two-man crew bailed out after arming the explosives, and the plane was flown by remote control from the trailing plane and guided to the target. The program was a complete disaster. Only one plane ever hit its target; the rest all crashed. Unfortunately, the explosives on Kennedy's plane detonated prematurely.

After John F. Kennedy was assassinated, his brother, Attorney General Robert F. Kennedy, barred recently sworn-in President Lyndon B. Johnson from the Oval Office for several days, as he conspired to keep Johnson from assuming control of the government.

OLD HICKORY

Andrew Jackson's wife, Rachel, committed bigamy when she married him, as she was already married.

Jackson fought thirteen duels defending his wife's honor. In 1806, he killed a man in a duel and received a bullet wound to his chest.

Jackson was a very poor speller.

When he served in the House of Representatives, he voted against a resolution to honor George Washington.

Jackson, an enthusiastic "Indian hunter," picked up the nickname "Old Hickory" on a march home with his troops, when he let a sick soldier have his horse while he walked. Hickory was the toughest wood his men could think of to call him.

After Jackson's troops had killed many Native Americans in one battle, he adopted a Native American infant boy whose parents did not survive the battle.

BARRY BASICS

Barack Obama was known as "Barry" in his youth, but asked that he be called by his given name "Barack," when he entered college.

Obama speaks Indonesian, which he learned as a child in Indonesia.

Barack Obama and Warren Buffet are seventh cousins, three times removed. They share a common ancestor—a Frenchman from the 1650s.

Obama claims he may be a distant relative of Jefferson Davis, president of the Confederate States of America.

Obama met his future wife, Michelle Robinson, in 1989, while he was a summer associate at a Chicago law firm and she was assigned to mentor him.

Michelle's brother is Craig Robinson, coach of the Oregon State University basketball team.

RUTHER*FRAUD* B. HAYES

Rutherford B. Hayes, the Republican candidate, won the presidential election of 1876 even though his opponent, Democrat Samuel Tilden, won the popular vote by 250,000 votes. At the close of the polls, Tilden had 184 electoral votes and Hayes had 165. Four states—Florida, Oregon, Louisiana, and South Carolina (with twenty total electoral votes)—were too close to call. A special commission was set up to decide the matter, consisting of seven Democrats, seven Republicans and one Independent. At the last minute, the Independent stepped down and was replaced by a Republican. All twenty votes, and the election, went to Hayes.

The only reason the Democrats went along with the skewed vote is because the Republicans promised that Hayes would only serve one term and they would remove federal troops that still occupied the heavily Democratic South after the Civil War. Both promises were kept.

Hayes was inaugurated in a secret ceremony because outgoing President Grant feared there might be an insurrection by Tilden supporters.

For the next four years, Democrats referred to the president as Rutherfraud B. Hayes.

THIRD-PLACE PRESIDENT

William Howard Taft was the last sitting president to run for reelection and finish third in the Electoral College.

ONE AND DONE

President John Tyler Jr. was thrown out of his Whig Party while in office for twice vetoing a bill they had passed through Congress. He had no party affiliation after this and was thus unable to realistically run for reelection.

After leaving office, Tyler was elected to the House of Representatives of the Confederate Congress during the Civil War, but died before taking office.

Because Tyler sided with the South, his passing was not officially mourned.

BEST PRESIDENT YOU KNOW THE LEAST ABOUT

President James K. Polk was probably the most accessible American president. Twice each week he would receive visits from the general public at the White House. All one had to do was show up and present his card to the doorman, and Polk would take a meeting with him.

During his administration, the United States acquired Texas, Washington State, Idaho, Oregon, California, Nevada, Utah, Arizona, and parts of Wyoming, Colorado, and New Mexico.

Polk tried unsuccessfully to buy Cuba from Spain.

> After serving one term, Polk had accomplished every goal he promised to achieve, and he retired without seeking reelection. He died from cholera three months later.

WEST WING WISE

The British only occupied Washington, DC, for about twenty-six hours after burning down the White House during the War of 1812, since a hurricane *and* a tornado hit the city shortly thereafter, killing many British troops and badly damaging their guns and ships.

> After the burning of the White House, the country's leaders considered moving the capital to Cincinnati, which was too far inland to be susceptible to a surprise attack.

The West Wing of the White House was damaged by fire again in 1929.

> The White House is the only world leader's home that is open to the public.

Today's White House pressroom was FDR's swimming pool room until Nixon took office.

> The third floor was added during the Hoover administration.

Before Teddy Roosevelt started putting "White House" on his stationary in 1901, the building was officially known as the Executive Mansion.

Harry Truman had the whole building gutted and renovated in 1949.

The White House is painted with Whisper White by Duron.

CAPITOL IDEA

The U.S. Capitol Building served as a military hospital during the Civil War. So did the Smithsonian Institute.

The first capital for the Congress of the Confederation, America's first governing body after declaring independence, was in Philadelphia. In 1783, members of the Continental Army mutinied outside of the capital and demanded back pay owed them. Congress fled Philly and set up temporarily in Princeton, New Jersey, then moved to Annapolis, Maryland, and then to Trenton, New Jersey, before settling in New York in 1785.

The U.S. Capitol was originally going to be called "Congress Hall," but Thomas Jefferson insisted it be named the "Capitol," after "Capitoline Hill," site of a Roman temple to Jupiter Optimus Maximus.

Slave labor did much of the work of expanding the Capitol building in the 1850s.

The first recorded attempt to kill a U.S. president occurred at the Capitol, when in 1835 a man pulled two pistols on President Andrew Jackson, both of which misfired. The assailant was subdued by Congressmen, including Davy Crockett. Jackson reputedly beat the man with his cane.

In 1915, a German professor detonated a bomb in the Senate chamber because he wanted to prevent America from siding with the Allies in World War I.

In 1954, members of Congress were shot at by Puerto Rican nationalists.

In 1971, the radical group the Weather Underground set off a bomb in the Capitol to protest U.S. involvement in Laos.

In 1983, a radical group called the Armed Resistance exploded a bomb outside the office of Senate Minority leader Robert Byrd to protest the American intervention in Grenada.

In 1998, a deranged man opened fire at the Capitol, killing two security guards.

It is believed that the Capitol Building was the intended target of 9/11 Flight 93, which crashed in western Pennsylvania.

IF YOU CAN'T BEAT THEM

In 1856, an antislavery U.S. Senator from Massachusetts—Charles Sumner—was beaten so severely with a cane by a pro-slavery Congressman—Preston Brooks—on the Senate floor, that he needed three years to recover from his head trauma. Brooks's accomplice in this crime was fellow South Carolina congressman Laurence Keitt, who waved a pistol and refused to let anyone help Sumner. Brooks took exception to a speech Sumner had made that attacked both slavery and him personally. Brooks amazingly survived an expulsion vote in the House and was reelected by his constituents, who considered him a hero. Keitt was censured by the House

BOOK BURNINGS

The Library of Congress was burned three times. The first time was in 1814, when it was housed in the U.S. Capitol building, which the British set afire. The second and third fires, in 1825 and 1851 respectively, also occurred while the library resided within the Capitol. The 1851 fire destroyed two-thirds of the collection, some thirty-five thousand books.

In 1897, the Library of Congress moved into its own building.

Today, the Library of Congress contains 144 million items.

CHICAGO DALEY NEWS

Richard J. Daley held the record for tenure as mayor of Chicago at twenty-one years. His son, Richard M. Daley, surpassed his father's time in office in December 2010.

WELCOME TO THE MACHINE

Tammany Hall was the name of New York's corrupt political machine, which controlled Democratic politics in the city from 1830 until the 1960s. They were also known as the Tammany Society (after Lenape leader Tamanend). When the society built a hall for their group in 1830 on East 14th Street, the name became synonymous with the society and the building.

William "Boss" Tweed was the leader of Tammany Hall in 1870 and as commissioner of public works stole between $40 million and $200 million (between $1.5 and $8 billion in today's money). Tweed was convicted and imprisoned in 1872. He escaped custody and fled to Spain, where he worked as a seaman. He was eventually caught and returned to debtor's prison in New York, where he died in 1878.

WE THE PEOPLE . . .

The U.S. Constitution was written by Protestants.

As of late 2010, there are no Protestants on the Supreme Court.

Two out of three Americans surveyed cannot name one Supreme Court Justice.

Since 1953, nine Supreme Court justices have been graduates of Harvard Law School, six from Yale Law School, and two each from Columbia, Northwestern, and Stanford.

The Constitution specifically allowed the continued importation of slaves for twenty years after ratification, prohibited helping escaped slaves, and defined slaves as "three-fifths" of a person.

Rhode Island refused to send delegates to the Constitutional Convention.

Notable patriots absent from the convention included Patrick Henry, John Adams, Samuel Adams, and John Hancock.

CONTEMPTIBLE COURT

In the 1857 *Dred Scott v. Sandford* case, the U.S. Supreme Court ruled that slaves, even those living in free states, were the property of their owners and could never become citizens, and thus had no legal standing to sue for their freedom.

Plessy v. Ferguson in 1896 found that segregated facilities for blacks and whites were constitutional.

Francis v. Resweber was brought by convicted killer Willie Francis in 1946, after the State of Louisiana had botched his execution in the electric chair and planned to "re-execute" him. The court found that this did not constitute double jeopardy and was not cruel and unusual punishment. Francis was executed the following year.

Coker v. Georgia found that the death penalty is not a constitutional punishment for the rape of an adult woman.

Korematsu v. United States in 1994 found that it was okay to round up and confine Americans of Japanese ancestry during World War II.

Kelo v. City of New London in 2005 found that the government can take property from one private individual and give it to another to further "economic development." In this case, New London, Connecticut, wanted to seize a nine-acre neighborhood and find a developer to build condos, a hotel, and a shopping center on the property. All the homeowners were driven out, and today their land sits vacant.

Buck v. Bell (1927) upheld the forced sterilization of the mentally ill. Justice Oliver Wendell Holmes said, "Three generations of imbeciles are enough."

Lochner v. New York (1905) ruled that states could not pass laws restricting the number of hours that companies had their employees work.

LAW AND DISORDER

G-MEN

The FBI has offices in sixty different foreign countries.

The FBI is one of thirty-two different agencies with law enforcement responsibilities in the United States.

The FBI receives thirty-four thousand new fingerprint cards daily.

Originally, the Bureau only investigated white-collar crimes, and agents were accountants and lawyers. When their duties were expanded to control the interstate crime sprees occurring in the Midwest in the early 1930s, the accountants and lawyers had to quickly learn how to handle firearms and become actual policemen.

G-MAN

J. Edgar Hoover was the Director of the Federal Bureau of Investigation for forty-eight years. He started out as a clerk in the Justice Department.

The FBI agents under Hoover reported only to Hoover. The attorney general and even the president had no control over them.

Hoover investigated and kept extensive files on tens of thousands of Americans he considered "subversives." This gave him great power over politicians, the media, and Hollywood.

It was his secret files, including compromising photos, that kept him in power through eight different presidents. They all were afraid to fire him, not knowing what he had on them.

Hoover had to approve any film or TV script featuring the FBI and even had veto power over which actors appeared in such projects.

Because of Hoover's abuse of power while director, present-day directors are limited to tenures of ten years.

PUBLIC ENEMY NUMBER ONE

In the early 1930s, the FBI came up with its Public Enemies list in response to the many violent gangs of criminals roaming the Midwest at the time.

John Dillinger was the first Public Enemy Number One.

John Dillinger would sometimes case prospective banks to rob by impersonating an alarm company salesman and assessing their security system and vault. Other times he would pose as a movie producer scouting locations for a bank robbery scene.

Dillinger's gang actually robbed police stations when they needed more guns and ammunition.

Dillinger once escaped from jail using a "gun" he had made out of a piece of wood. He locked up all the guards in a cell and drove off in the sheriff's brand-new car.

Dillinger was shot dead outside a Chicago movie house in 1934, after having watched the gangster movie *Manhattan Melodrama*, starring Clark Gable.

After the death of John Dillinger, Baby Face Nelson became Public Enemy Number One.

Baby Face holds the dubious record of having killed more federal law enforcement agents than any other person.

Contrary to popular fiction, Ma Barker was not a gangster, although her sons were. She was never more than an accomplice.

Ma was killed in a shootout with the FBI in a Florida home in 1935. Although a tommy gun was found in her hands, it is believed the Feds put it there so they wouldn't be accused of killing a defenseless old lady.

Machine Gun Kelly's real name was George Kelly Barnes. Kelly acquired his famous moniker from his favorite choice of weapon—the Thompson machine gun.

Kelly's most famous crime was the kidnapping of oil tycoon Charles Urschel in 1933, which earned his gang a $200,000 ransom (the largest ever paid up until that time).

Unlike other famous gangsters of the time who died in a blaze of glory, Kelly surrendered peacefully to the FBI in 1933.

It is believed that he or his girlfriend first used the term "G-men," referring to the Feds during their arrest.

Charles Arthur "Pretty Boy" Floyd picked up his nickname after a bank clerk described the robber as being a "pretty boy with apple cheeks."

Floyd's most infamous alleged crime was his involvement in the Kansas City Massacre, where he and accomplices gunned down four lawmen and a felon they were transporting at the Union Railway Station in Kansas City, Missouri, in 1933.

Before meeting Clyde Barrow, Bonnie Parker was an honor roll student in high school.

Parker was married at age fifteen. Although she never saw her husband again after the end of their two-year marriage, she never divorced him and never removed her wedding ring.

The first man Clyde Barrow killed was his Texas prison cellmate who had repeatedly raped him for more than a year.

While imprisoned, Clyde chopped off a toe to avoid being placed on work details.

Together, Bonnie and Clyde are believed to have been involved in the murders of thirteen people (mostly lawmen), the kidnapping of several more, and break-ins of various armories to obtain weapons and ammo.

There is some controversy as to whether Bonnie ever really fired guns at people.

THE ROCK

Five prisoners have escaped from Alcatraz prison in two separate attempts. Two men broke out of the Rock in 1937, and three in 1962. None were ever seen again, and authorities claimed that they must have drowned, but there is no proof to support this contention.

Alcatraz only served as a prison for twenty-nine years, from 1934 through 1963.

In 1969, a group of Native Americans seized the island and held it for nineteen months, demanding reparations from the government for Indian lands seized in the past.

One and a half million tourists visit Alcatraz every year.

TAKE THIS PLANE TO CUBA!

Between 1968 and 1977, 414 airplanes were hijacked worldwide.

The only unsolved case involving a hijacked American plane is the case of "D.B. Cooper," an unknown man who hijacked a Northwest Orient plane flying from Portland, Oregon, to Seattle, Washington, in 1971. Cooper parachuted from the back of the plane with $200,000 in ransom money and was never seen again.

Four months after the Cooper incident, Richard McCoy Jr. hijacked a United Airlines flight in Denver, Colorado. He demanded $500,000 and, like Cooper, parachuted out of the back of the plane, over Utah. Unlike Cooper, he left enough clues behind to incriminate himself and was arrested two days later. In 1974, McCoy escaped from prison and remained on the lam for three months until he was shot to death by an FBI agent in a shoot-out in Virginia.

In 1974, American Samuel Byck tried to hijack a Delta flight and crash it into the White House to kill President Richard Nixon. Byck shot and killed a terminal guard at Baltimore/Washington International Airport and stormed aboard a plane on the runway. He then entered the cockpit and demanded the pilots take off. When told they couldn't do so until the blocks were removed from the wheels, Byck shot and killed one pilot and wounded the other. He then grabbed a female passenger and told her to fly the plane. A police officer fired four shots through the cockpit door, wounding Byck, who then shot himself.

In 1972, three men hijacked a Southern Airlines plane using guns and grenades and threatened to fly it into Oak Ridge National Laboratory if they didn't receive $10 million. After wounding the copilot and flying to multiple destinations, they were arrested by police after landing in Havana, Cuba.

In 1986, four Palestinian terrorists, disguised as airport security, stormed aboard a Pan Am flight on the runway in Karachi, Pakistan. The pilot, copilot, and engineer escaped out an emergency hatch in the cockpit. When Pakistani security forces prepared to storm the plane, the hijackers killed twenty-one passengers and injured more than 150 before being arrested. They received life sentences but were released from prison by the Pakistani government in 2008, despite the objections of the United States. In 2009, the FBI offered a $5 million reward for information leading to their capture.

In 1994, a FedEx employee, Auburn Calloway, attempted to hijack a plane using hammers and a spear gun. Calloway, who was about to be dismissed for lying on his resume, tried to neutralize the three-man crew by assaulting them with the hammers. He then planned to fly the plane into the FedEx headquarters in Memphis, Tennessee. Calloway planned for the deaths of the crew to look consistent with blunt force trauma from the crash, entitling his family to collect on the $2.5 million life insurance policy FedEx had for its employees killed while at work. However, the crew was able to overpower Calloway, even though each suffered massive head wounds. It was only by the captain performing extreme aerial maneuvers to keep Calloway off balance that the crew was able to subdue him. None of the crew is physically fit to fly any longer.

STICK 'EM UP!

In 1950, the Brinks headquarters in Boston was robbed of $2 million. The crime went unsolved for over six years, until one of the eleven thieves ratted out the others on a plea deal for an unrelated offense. The others were indicted just four days before the statute of limitations expired.

> In the Great Train Robbery of 1963, a British Royal Mail train was emptied of over $7 million in bank notes. Twelve of the fifteen crooks were arrested shortly afterward when their fingerprints were found in their hideout. One of them, Ronnie Biggs, escaped prison in 1965, had plastic surgery in Paris, and eluded capture in Australia and Brazil. He voluntarily surrendered to British authorities in 2001.

A group affiliated with the Palestine Liberation Organization blew out the walls of the British Bank of the Middle East in 1976, getting away with approximately

$50 million worth of gold, jewelry, and currency. Yasser Arafat reportedly chartered a plane and took millions of dollars to Switzerland to deposit in a secret account.

Known as the Lufthansa Heist, $6 million in cash and $1 million in jewels was stolen from a storage area at JFK Airport in New York in 1978. The culprits were never caught, but police suspect "Jimmy the Gent" Burke, a mobster portrayed by Robert De Niro in the movie *Goodfellas*, was behind the heist.

In 1983, Victor Manuel Gerena, a guard at the Wells Fargo armored truck depot in West Hartford, Connecticut, pulled a gun on two of his coworkers, handcuffed and drugged them, and made off with $7 million in cash in the trunk of his car. He is believed to have fled to Mexico and then Cuba. He still remains on the FBI's Ten Most Wanted list with a reward offered of $1 million.

In 1987, two men entered the Knightsbridge Safe Deposit Centre in Westminster, England, and requested to rent a safe deposit box. When the manager showed them into the vault, they subdued him and the guards, hung up a sign saying the center was temporarily closed, and looted an estimated $98 million from the boxes. This was the largest bank robbery up until that time. The culprits were all later arrested.

Two guys dressed as cops duct-taped two security guards at Boston's Isabella Stewart Garden Museum on St. Patrick's Day 1990 and made off with $300 million worth of paintings by Degas, Rembrandt, and Manet. The museum's surveillance video was taken by the crooks before they left. The robbers were never caught, and the artwork is still missing.

The largest cash robbery in U.S. history was the 1997 Dunbar Armored robbery in Los Angeles that netted almost $20 million. It was an inside job, and cops cracked the case when one of the robbers stupidly gave someone a stack of bills still wrapped in the original cash strap. Less than half of the money was recovered.

In 2005, thieves tunneled under two city blocks and blasted through three feet of reinforced concrete to get inside of Brazil's Banco Central's vault, taking $65 million. That much money weighs 7,700 pounds. The bank hadn't insured the money because they felt the risk of loss didn't justify the premiums. Nine million dollars of the loot, along with some of the perpetrators, has been recovered.

In something right out of a movie, thieves hovered in a stolen helicopter over the roof of the GS4 cash depot in Sweden in 2009 as men rappelled onto the roof, smashed through glass skylights, bombed their way through walls into the vault, and hoisted out about $150 million in cash. Police were unable to pursue the gang in their own helicopter because the robbers had left a bomb in front of the police helicopter hangar. The investigation is still ongoing.

In 2010, an Iraqi bank was relieved of $5.5 million after its guards were served tea that had been laced with a strong sleep-inducing drug.

UNLUCKY LINDY

The kidnapping of Charles Lindbergh's twenty-month-old son, Charles Augustus Lindbergh Jr., in 1932 prompted Congress to pass the Lindbergh Law, making it a federal offense to take a kidnap victim across state lines and to use the mail in the commission of the crime or in the demanding of a ransom.

ALL BY MYSELF

There are presently eighty thousand Americans in solitary confinement.

Typically, inmates held in solitary spend twenty-three hours a day there.

It costs twice as much to keep a prisoner in solitary.

TIME SERVED

Al Capone served seven and a half years of his tax evasion conviction.

Sarah Jane Moore, who tried to shoot President Gerald Ford in 1975, was paroled in 2007 after serving thirty-two years of a life sentence.

Lynette "Squeaky" Fromme, who also tried to kill Ford in 1975, was paroled in 2009 after serving thirty-four years of a life sentence, even though she continued to threaten Ford while in prison and escaped for two days in 1987 to try to meet up with Charles Manson. During one hearing, she beaned U.S. Attorney Duane Keyes in the head with an apple.

DR. DEATH

Dr. Jack Kevorkian served eight years of a ten-to-twenty-five year sentence for assisting in 130 suicides.

> Assisted suicides are now legal, in some cases, in Oregon and Washington.

E-CRIMINALS

Washington, DC, has the most "e-criminals" per capita in the United States. (An e-criminal is someone who uses the Internet for credit card fraud, e-commerce theft, identity theft, cyberstalking, child pornography, etc.) Nevada and Washington State come in second and third.

THE WAY WE WERE

YOUR NAME IS MUDD

Before John Wilkes Booth assassinated President Abraham Lincoln on Good Friday, April 14, 1865, he tried to kidnap him and ransom him for the return of Confederate POWs held in the North. When Lincoln announced that he wanted to extend the right to vote to blacks, Booth decided to kill the president instead.

The plot to murder Lincoln was part of a larger conspiracy. That same night, Lewis Powell repeatedly stabbed Secretary of State William Seward while he slept in his bed. Seward would have been killed, but he was recuperating from a serious carriage accident at the time, and a jaw splint he was wearing prevented the knife from cutting his jugular vein. Seward's children and nurse were also injured in the attack.

George Atzerodt was supposed to kill Vice President Andrew Johnson but chickened out.

General Ulysses S. Grant was also to have been killed at Ford's Theatre, where Lincoln was murdered, but he changed his plans at the last minute and didn't go.

The manhunt for Booth was the largest in world history up till that time.

Contrary to popular myth, Dr. Samuel Mudd, who tended Booth's broken leg and was sentenced to life in prison, is not the source of the expression "your name is mud."

Mudd was pardoned by President Andrew Johnson after serving four years at Fort Jefferson in the Dry Tortugas (off Key West, Florida).

Lincoln found no peace in death. In 1876, two counterfeiters were caught in the act of stealing his corpse from a cemetery in Springfield, Illinois. They had planned to ransom it for the release of a fellow counterfeiter from prison.

Between 1865 and 1901, Lincoln's coffin was opened six different times for various reasons.

IF AT FIRST YOU DON'T SECEDE . . .

The Confederacy had no political parties.

Jefferson Davis was a U.S. senator who voted against secession.

Jefferson Davis married future president General Zachary Taylor's daughter, Sarah Knox Taylor, against his wishes. She died three months later from malaria.

Davis was elected unopposed for a six-year term to be the President of the Confederate States of America.

In the last days of the Civil War, Davis and others had a plan to flee to Cuba and regroup. At the war's end, he was indicted for treason and imprisoned. While in jail, he sold his Mississippi estate to one of his former slaves.

MR. X

Malcolm X was born Malcolm Little. After he joined the Nation of Islam, he changed his surname to "X," which was supposed to represent the true African family name of his forebears that he could never know. He considered Little his "slave" name. He was also known as El-Hajj Malik El-Shabazz.

Malcolm X referred to Martin Luther King Jr. as a "chump."

Malcolm X had six daughters. One was named Attallah, after Attila the Hun, and one named Qubilah, after Kublai Khan.

PAINE IN THE BUTTON

Thomas Paine, author of *Common Sense*, is the first person to use the words "the United States of America."

Paine died a destitute drunk. Only six people went to his funeral.

Ten years after his death, his body was exhumed by an admirer and shipped to England to be placed in a fitting memorial. The funds were never raised, and his remains were stored in a trunk in an attic until they disappeared from history. Some say his bones were sold to make buttons.

TRAINED ORPHANS

The Orphan Train movement, which ran from 1854 through 1929, took orphaned and abused children from the streets of New York and other cities and put them on trains to pioneer families in the American West. When the children arrived in a town, they were paraded before the public and interested townspeople could pick the ones they wanted. The children became indentured servants of their new families. They were not adopted and had no birth certificates. Upon reaching the age of eighteen, they were free to leave. Boys received $150 and girls $50 from the movement. Two hundred thousand American children were eventually relocated by the Orphan Trains.

ROAD TRIP

The first person to drive across America was Dr. Horatio Nelson Jackson in 1903. His San Francisco–to–New York City road trip, which took sixty-four days, was achieved at a time when there were fewer than 150 miles of paved roads in the United States, no road maps, and virtually no gas stations along the way.

HOLY TOLEDO

The Ohio-Michigan War of 1835–36 was the result of the state of Ohio and the territory of Michigan both claiming a strip of land that included Toledo. Both sides raised militias and did a lot of saber rattling. Ohio blocked Michigan's admission to the Union. To resolve the matter, Congress gave the "Toledo Strip" to Ohio and compensated Michigan by giving it the Upper Peninsula and allowing it into the Union.

During the dispute, folks in Ohio disparaged folks from Michigan by calling them "wolverines." Michiganders took a liking to the label and named their new state the Wolverine State. (There are no wolverines in Michigan.)

SEW WHAT?

Isaac Merritt Singer, of sewing machine fame, fathered eighteen children with four different women.

In the 1950s, three-quarters of American homes had sewing machines; now, only about 5 percent do.

MARCO POLO OF AMERICA

Between 1528 and 1536, Spaniard Cabeza de Vaca led an expedition that crossed what is now the Southwestern United States and reached the Pacific on foot. He was enslaved by Native Americans for two years of that time and did most of his exploring in the nude, as he had used his clothing building and repairing primitive boats early in his adventure.

> The second person to traverse North America and reach the Pacific was Scotsman Sir Alexander Mackenzie, who traveled across Canada by canoe and reached the Pacific in 1793.

The Lewis and Clark Expedition was the third transcontinental crossing of North America. Only one member of the thirty-three-person party died during the trip, from acute appendicitis.

> During the journey, Meriwether Lewis was shot in the leg by a nearsighted member of the expedition who mistook him for an elk.

DEAL OF THE CENTURY

When France lost Haiti and its lucrative sugar trade, it no longer needed the wheat fields of the Midwest that fed all its slave labor on the island. This was a deciding factor when France agreed to sell the Louisiana Territory to the United States.

> The Louisiana Purchase was the largest land transaction in world history.

THE GOOD OL' DAYS

A century ago, Americans lived very differently than they do today:

Only 13.5 percent of Americans had graduated from high school.

Most women only washed their hair once a month.

More than 95 percent of births occurred at home.

In 1904, there were only 144 miles of paved roads in the United States. Today there are about 2.7 million miles of paved roads.

RIDING THE RAILS

In 1920, there were 2 million railroad employees in the United States. In 2004, there were just 170,000.

Each railroad kept its own time, usually based on the time the sun was highest in the sky above its headquarters city. Thus, railway stations had many clocks, each showing a different time, one for each railroad that used the station.

WELCOME TO AMERICA

About one-half of Americans can trace an ancestor who came through Ellis Island.

Part of Ellis Island belongs to New York, but the bulk of it belongs to New Jersey.

Immigrants landing at Ellis Island received an initial six-second medical exam. If doctors noted any potential problems, they marked the immigrants' clothes with a code letter in chalk, indicating what was suspected and that further examination was required.

NOMADIC HORDES

Enormous swarms of Rocky Mountain locusts, one larger in area than the state of California, covered the skies and devastated the croplands on the Great Plains in the 1870s. The number of insects in the largest swarm is estimated to have been 12.5 trillion.

The locusts sharply declined shortly afterward, as their breeding grounds were destroyed by cattle and agriculture. They were extinct thirty years later.

A BRIEF HISTORY
OF THE WORLD

SPARE PARTS

In 1087, men hired by the Italian town of Bari stole the bones of St. Nicholas (better known as St. Nick) from Myra, in present-day Turkey. The relics, which still reside in Bari, were believed to exude myrrh.

The U.S. military kept part of Benito Mussolini's brain after his death in 1945. The government returned the gray matter to Mussolini's widow in 1966.

OFF WITH THEIR HEADS!

During the 1937 Great Purge in the Soviet Union, Joseph Stalin had thirty thousand of his military officers executed, leaving the armed forces in chaos.

During the French Reign of Terror from 1793 to 1794, about forty thousand citizens lost their heads.

DON'T CRY FOR ME

Eva Perón, more commonly known as Evita, died of cancer when she was only thirty-three. After her death, Evita's embalmed corpse was displayed for viewing for two years. A huge memorial statue, bigger than the Statue of Liberty, was planned to house her body. Unfortunately, her husband, Juan Perón, was overthrown by a military dictatorship and fled the country, leaving her corpse behind. The new regime banned all things Perón. It was illegal to have a picture of Juan or Evita, or to even speak their names. Evita's body disappeared for sixteen years. In 1971, Juan discovered its whereabouts in Milan, Italy, and had it delivered to his home in Spain, where he was still in exile. He was elected to the presidency of Argentina in 1973 and died in 1974. Perón's third wife, who assumed the presidency when he died, had Evita's corpse flown back to Argentina, where it remains today.

LONDON BRIDGE IS FALLING DOWN

There has been a bridge over the Thames at the site of London Bridge since the Romans erected one in AD 50.

The little settlement that sprang up next to the bridge was called Londinium.

London Bridge was destroyed by a tornado in 1091 and again in 1136 by a fire.

The rebuilding of the bridge was subsidized by two hundred shops and houses built right on the bridge.

In 1212, simultaneous fires started at both ends of the bridge, trapping and killing about three thousand people in the middle.

London Bridge was sold to American Robert P. Mc-Colloch in 1968 for $2,460,000. It was reassembled at Lake Havasu City, Arizona, and is now the state's second most popular tourist attraction, after the Grand Canyon.

Tower Bridge, the one with the two huge towers at either end, is often confused with London Bridge. It is of more recent construction (1886) and is the next bridge downstream from London Bridge.

DEADLY SKIES

The deadliest plane crash was that of Japan Airlines Flight 123 in 1985, from Tokyo to Osaka, which killed 520 of the 524 people on board.

In 1983, Korean Airlines Flight 007, en route from New York City to Seoul, South Korea, was shot down by Soviet MiG fighters when it strayed into Soviet airspace, killing all 269 on board.

There have been fourteen different lone survivors of major plane crashes. The majority of them were children.

CABLE NEWS

The transatlantic telegraph cable cut the time for messages between Europe and the United States down from ten days to mere minutes.

Five attempts were made at laying the cable before a successful cable was put into use in 1866. The first cable, laid in 1857, burned out after only one month, when excessive voltage through the line was used while trying to increase telegraph speed.

Undersea cables were still used until satellite communication became possible in the 1960s.

HOLIER THAN THOU

Mother Teresa was born Agnesë Gonxhe Bojaxhiu.

At eighteen, she left her family to become a nun and never saw them again.

Teresa was an Albanian with Indian citizenship.

There are more than ten thousand Roman Catholic saints.

Among other requirements, two miracles are needed to become a saint. One of them must be posthumous.

The Catholic Church maintains that it does not make people saints, but rather "recognizes" them.

AROUND THE WORLD IN *SEVENTY-TWO* DAYS

In 1888, a newspaper reporter named Nellie Bly traveled around the world in seventy-two days to beat Jules Verne's fictional Phineas Fogg, protagonist of the 1873 novel, *Around the World in Eighty Days*. Bly, however, made the trip alone.

HENRY THE EIGHTH I AM

Henry VIII weighed almost four hundred pounds when he died.

> When Henry began putting on weight later in his life, members of his court padded their clothes to look more like him.

Henry VIII was responsible for the beheadings and other deaths of more than seventy thousand English subjects.

RETURN TO SENDER

The United Kingdom issued the first postage stamps in 1840—the penny black and the two-pence blue.

> Before this, the recipient was responsible for paying for mail, not the sender.

In those days, folks did not use envelopes. Letters were folded and sealed with the address and stamp on the backside.

The United Kingdom is the only country that does not put its name on its stamps, but rather features an image of the sovereign instead.

OUT IN THE COLD

Englishman Robert F. Scott believed he would be the first person to reach the South Pole. However, when he arrived there on January 17, 1912, he found a tent with a note from Norwegian Roald Amundsen explaining that he had beaten Scott there by a mere thirty-five days. Scott and his group froze to death on the return trip across the ice. Their bodies were not found for eight months.

Amundsen died in a plane crash while on a rescue mission to locate an airship that had crashed in the Arctic Ocean in 1928. His body and plane were never found.

Amundsen was also the first person to successfully navigate the Northwest Passage from the Atlantic Ocean to the Pacific Ocean, sailing the waters north of Canada. It took him three years, from 1903 to 1906, as he spent three winters trapped in ice.

GREAT MOMENTS IN HISTORY

The lever voting machine was invented by Jacob H. Myers and first used in Lockport, New York, in 1892. It had more moving parts then almost any other machine of the time.

German Andreas Stihl invented the first chainsaw in 1926.

The 33⅓ record was introduced in 1948.

In 1955, 45s began to outsell 78s.

BAH HUMBUG

Christmas was banned in Scotland for four hundred years until the 1950s, because the Presbyterian Church back then considered it a "Papist" or Catholic day. It didn't become a public holiday until 1958.

ACKNOWLEDGMENTS

As always, many thanks to my editor, Jeanette Shaw, whose expert hand guided this series from the very beginning. To Andy Ball for the painstaking work required to fact-check a book with this much information. It's reassuring to have their support. To Sarah Romeo for coming up with such a clever photomontage on the cover. And of course to my literary agent, Janet Rosen, whose enthusiasm for my writing and skilled representation truly are "indespensable."